COVERT MANIPULATION

BLOWING THEIR COVERS!

Learn How Manipulation Works & How to Defend Yourself from Manipulative People

ROBERT MOORE

"The best lightning rod for your protection is your own spine."

— Ralph Waldo Emerson

consent of the author or copyright owner. Legal action will be pursued if this is breached.

Disclaimer Notice:

Please note the information contained within this document is for educational and entertainment purposes only. Every attempt has been made to provide accurate, up to date and reliable complete information. No warranties of any kind are expressed or implied. Readers acknowledge that the author is not engaging in the rendering of legal, financial, medical or professional advice.

By reading this document, the reader agrees that under no circumstances are we responsible for any losses, direct or indirect, which are incurred as a result of the use of information contained within this document, including, but not limited to, —errors, omissions, or inaccuracies.

TABLE OF CONTENTS

INTRODUCTION

"No boundary or barrier surrounds the heart of a person that loves their self and others."

— Shannon L. Alder

BUILDING BOUNDARIES

First of all, think of this book as an extreme makeover holistically, not with buff, bulging muscles, a new wardrobe, and a hot haircut, but with a total transformation of your mind! As Adler remarks in the above quote, we must engage in self-love in order to be totally free. When we are free, nothing or no one can stop us from succeeding or living our best lives, not even clever, cunning, covert manipulators. As a result, this book is essentially all about breaking free of victims' labels, past manipulations, present webs of deception and woe, barricades bullying, malicious mind control mechanisms, and/or feelings of overall powerlessness. We can learn how to self-protect ourselves and our loved ones in a positive, proactive, productive way today. Walls and fences are quite easy to erect, but boundaries are much more daunting to build and maintain, right? Channel your inner Bob the Builder and let's dig in to explore more about this critical topic. Based on this book's lessons, you can begin to *blow the covers off* covert manipulation!

> *"You can either be a victim of the world or an adventurer in search of treasure. It all depends on how you view your life."*
> — *Paulo Coelho, Eleven Minutes*

Stop being a victim, as the above quote suggests. I know this advice sounds simple and perhaps even a bit harsh. What does this vital message really entail? It encourages us to turn our tragedies, as Coelho advises in the quote above, into treasures. Take the messy, ugly, shameful, painful, and unspeakable pasts and parts of us and begin to see how resilient and strong they have made us.

Specifically, part of this massive transformation directly involves your mind (and words!). Save the labels for the soup cans and quit calling yourself a victim right now. Start proclaiming yourself as the powerful, courageous, resilient person you are and are meant to be!

Are you tired of constantly being a victim from others' manipulative schemes, bullying antics, petty plots, and malicious maneuvers at home, while dating, during work, within friendships, and/or among everyday family fiascos and scandals? Do you feel lately that your life has become more like a reality show or game? Have you been hurt socioemotionally, spiritually, physically, sexually, and/or psychologically by another person's conniving games, false facades, or evil personas? Were you ever misled financially and/or politically? If you can relate to these questions, then this book will allow you to take back your power and life.

Why is manipulation the norm lately, or so it seems? We live in a world presently where pyramid schemes, cheating scandals, money laundering, stolen identities, and other alarming acts foster the need for us to explore how manipulators operate in order to guard ourselves and find ways to deflect these conniving efforts. For these reasons, this book will allow you to *blow the covers off covert manipulators*, so you can protect better yourself and your loved ones proactively.

Accordingly, I will also help you to learn how to establish and maintain loving, logical, and ethical boundaries at the same time. If you are still feeling like a *victim*, I want to direct your attention to a mini linguistics lesson that I created, one that already keeps me in a positive mindset to reassure me that I will persevere from the darkness. Be inspired that the last two letters in 'victim" are "I'M" to signify empowerment and resilience! Manipulators cannot win with that "I am" still in survivor mentality! You are still an "I am" and in this to win it in life!

ANALYZE YOUR EXPERIENCES WITH COVERT MANIPULATION: GROUNDHOG'S DAY DRAMA

Does your life often feel like the *Groundhog's Day* movie as far as endless exposures, repetitive tragedies, senseless schemes, and countless dramas from covert manipulators? Did someone cleverly disguise one's dark side under a colorful cloak of charm, charisma, eloquence, confidence, phoniness, and lies? Do you find yourself recurrently frustrated, stressed, depressed, anxious, angry and confused about why you are always targeted by cunning romantic partners, disloyal family members, benevolent strangers, nasty neighbors, and unapologetic bosses or co-workers?

Are you familiar with the loads of online and digital influencers nowadays? Soules (2015) in *Media, Persuasion and Propaganda* argues how we currently live amid such a massive era, a fast and furious, frenzied "age of persuasion, a century of applied research in advertising, advocacy, public relations, mass entertainment and social control." Even the popular practice of taking selfies seems to signify that people currently tend to care more about themselves right now than about the welfare of others, ethics, moral codes, laws, the environment, and other vital parts of life, right? Have you noticed lately have many selfie takers have actually fallen over cliffs and literally rolled into ravines to their own deaths just for a meager picture of themselves? This book seeks to ensure that you also do not allow manipulators to lure you to an early grave with their narcissistic nets.

ERA OF INFLUENCE

Yet how do we balance the flip side of persuasion while living in an era where influence, especially using technological and digital innovations, is so prominent? How do we manage strong, controlling personalities? What do we do with all the parades of persuasive and influential message around us? Which ones are legitimate and which are totally bogus? How can we stay float against all this media mind control?

If you are presently an online user or consumer of any kind or form, then you already know that there are indeed amazing merits that many digital influencers give, especially when we look at helpful media reviews, DIYs on YouTube, and other forms of social media information as power and knowledge. In this vein, "caring is sharing" as far as influence, but where is the line that we must straddle in order not to enter the dark abyss of manipulation and coercion? How do we not succumb to social control by and from others but instead tweak and channel some of their persuasive appeals and techniques smartly, morally, ethically, and proactively to our own personal advantages? These questions will be tackled throughout the course of this book.

> *"Perhaps what matters when all is said and done it's not who puts us down but who picks us up."*
> — *Kate DiCamillo, Louisiana's Way Home*

As echoed in DiCamillo's insightful quote above, my book radiates with research-based yet practical ways to make you more resilient from and after episodes with covert manipulation. We cannot expect life or others to pick us up after pain and tragedies strike us. We have to do it for ourselves, so be your own forklift after learning some valuable techniques and gaining increased knowledge and confidence from this book.

In sum, this book explores core concepts about mind control, human nature, personality types, the psychology of influence and manipulation, and other key themes. I will direct you how to learn to easily and confidently regulate your own life with more conviction, skills, confidence, communicative/interpersonal awareness, and control. This book will steer you in the right direction to take back your life after encountering a manipulator (or assisting you in avoiding one altogether). All in all, I strive to better hone your overall communicative and critical thinking skills, facilitate and sustain positive, healthy, human relationships, enrich your interpersonal aptitude, and easily enable you to achieve true health, security, love, happiness, and sanity. Sit back, as you open your mind, heart, and soul on this mindful and literary road trip. No toll payments are required!

TAKING THE WHEEL: HOW TO MOVE FROM BEING CONTROLLED TO IN CONTROL OF YOUR OWN LIFE?

"My life didn't please me, so I created my life."
— *Coco Chanel*

Do you want to create your own life makeover? Nope, I am not talking about new pair of jeans, a change of hair color to rainbow, or a new baseball cap. All in all, this book is practically designed to inform, explain, and empower with evidence and concepts, so you can identify covert manipulation by others. You will receive a ton of fun strategies and simple suggestions regarding how to proactively and effectively defend and assert yourself and your loved ones from manipulative people.

Whether you are sick of telemarketers scheming against you or currently caught in a vicious cycle of dating, hiring, marrying, and/or befriending antagonistic people, then this book can help you to become less of a human magnet for manipulators. I will even cover the topic of toxic leadership in this book, so you can shield yourself against any bad bosses, colleagues, clients, or supervisors out there. We'll let you take the *steering wheel* of your own life and fate accordingly. Buckle up and enjoy the ride with me-just no backseat driving, please!

> *"Life doesn't get easier or more forgiving, we get stronger and more resilient."*
> — *Steve Maraboli, Life, the Truth, and Being Free*

Why would I devote a book to a serious, controversial, often taboo topic, one that is often more Hollywood than self-help as far as mainstream misconceptions and stereotypes? Well, I have experienced some profound personal and professional deceptions from covert manipulators in my own work and school life and roles. These encounters have heavily hindered my productivity, shattered my confidence, and caused me to feel inferior, angry, lost, helpless, and alienated. I have also fallen for some covert manipulators in my romantic relationships and have wasted my time, money, and trust on some vile vixens. Do these episodes sound familiar to you as well?

I want you to reflect back truthfully. Were your childhood years, teen times, young adulthood experiences, or even more recent era more turbulent than terrific as far as your dealings with others? For me, the answer is yes to both. I also formerly lived under the wrath of some covert manipulators and dysfunctional family members during episodes of childhood dramas and traumas firsthand, so I want to help others to proactively, peacefully, logically, and autonomously defend, defy, recognize, and deal with covert manipulators with knowledge, empathy, logic, strength, and support.

Regardless of your past or present circumstances, this book is here in a proactive, peaceful, nonjudgmental manner. We all have likely had bumps in the road or even some major pot holes, but it's time to cruise beyond the pain and strain as we gain enlightenment and concrete techniques to fight back. We will gain resilience and support together against covert manipulation!

OVERVIEW TO CASE STUDY 1: WEDDING WOES

Another rationale for writing this book is that I recently befriended an inspirational American female from a professional work network. This mid-forties woman is now a highly educated, successful, popular, positive, attractive, cultured, optimistic, and spiritual person. She revealed to me how she was currently in a great second marriage with two amazing children. When I inquired about her first marriage, I could immediately sense the pain, embarrassment, and even terror on her face. She then confessed to me that she was formerly duped into an international marriage when she was younger and living abroad upon graduating from college for the first time in a drastically different culture.

Specifically, the manipulative man was not only extremely physically attractive to her from the get-go, "a real Casanova in the fairy tale sense," she alleged, but he was also "tall, dark, dreamy, and broodingly handsome" as far as his first impression. He was also highly cultured and extremely educated. This young woman, too, was intelligent, had two college degrees, was a former high school prom queen, hometown cheerleader, honor roll student, and coveted community leader back in America. She had dated quite a bit before and was not new to "courting," scene, as it was called in the 1990s. So how could someone of her status and even self-proclaimed feminism fall for such a schemer? What are the ways in which covert manipulators operate? How do they employ mind control tactics over us?

CASE STUDY 1 CONFESSIONS: ANALYZING A COVERT MANIPULATOR

"I have lost control over everything, even the places in my head."
— *Paula Hawkins, The Girl on the Train*

Hawkins' quote reiterates how loss of control is a major marker in any form of manipulative relationship. Let's look even closer at this covert manipulator's words, deeds, style, and tactics from the first case study. My female friend explained a bit more about the initial allure by this man. For example, she recalled how he had impressively spoken over five different languages fluently, had read over 500 books (yes, he was that meticulous and controlling that he even recorded each of them), was extremely outgoing, funny, beloved, and always "the life of the party!" She also elaborated how this man was a highly ranked officer in the military, extremely popular with others locally, deeply respected at his work and within the community, and one "heckuva listener," my friend recalled.

Are you noticing any tendencies yet or red flags? She then told me how he took advantage of her culture shock and adjustment struggles in a new place without any of her family, friends, or a support system. He listened with intent before we executed his perilous, multifaceted plan. Because of the vastly different climate, customs, foods, language, and norms in this new land, coupled with a highly stressful new job simultaneously, my friend recollected how she started to develop severe anxiety and numerous medical problems related to stress. She was eventually diagnosed with two autoimmune disorders, something that she still attributes today to the stress, trauma, and hazards that she faced from her dating and marriage to this manipulative menace.

"Narcissists are consumed with maintaining a shallow false self to others. They're emotionally crippled souls that are addicted to attention. Because of this they use a multitude of games, in order to receive adoration. Sadly, they are the most ungodly of God's creations because they don't show remorse for their actions, take steps to make amends or have empathy for others. They are morally bankrupt."

— Shannon L. Alder

As embedded in Adler's quote above, we will see "emotionally crippled" later as a recurrent theme when we talk about manipulators' lack of empathy as a common trait. Yet do you see any additional signs of "shallow false self to others" and "morally bankrupt" within the case study example yet? If not, then keep your eyes open as we explicate case study 1 a bit more for clues throughout the duration of this book. Don't worry, though, you will not need a magnifying glass, dark glasses, or secret spy hat on this psychological quest!

Now we will turn back to case study 1 to determine how to spot a manipulator. My friend divulged how due to a major health scare that required hospitalization, she then lost an excessive amount of weight, started to miss work frequently, had trouble keeping up with daily life like cleaning her apartment, paying her bills on time, getting groceries, and even getting out of bed. She was all alone in a strange place amid foreign social mores with no friends. Her colleagues were also aloof and totally oblivious to her problems because they were much older than she was and also from a different culture and language.

How did this manipulator manage to facilitate his fanaticism? First, this man became her one constant: he acted like a knight during her darkest days as he tried to nurse her back to health, taught her the new language and basic cultural customs, introduced her to locals and resources, and made her feel special. He bragged how he had so many connections and friends in this city that he would have her feeling like a local in no time.

She then wholeheartedly trusted his stories and lies. She allowed him to stay in her apartment and help her to physically and mentally recover. She liked him a lot, she stated, but she clarified to me that she did not love him romantically. She later learned that he was demonically drugging her all along when he was supposedly giving her herbal cures for her maladies. While she was impaired, he also took advantage of her intimately and sexually. He then started calling her his "soulmate" and began resorting to even more drastic measures to manipulate her further.

To illustrate, this devious, devilish man did not stop at stripping her mind, body, sexual power, spirit, faith, and finances, but he also caused her a major scandal at work and loss of reputation when the conservative locals learned that she was living as an unmarried woman with a man, a taboo that was vehemently shunned in the culture. He then paid a local nurse to alter my friend's pregnancy test, so the friend would falsely believe that she was having a baby with this man. The reality was that my friend had lost so much weight from her illnesses and stress that she had also misaligned her hormones and menstrual cycle.

Based on the baby lie that he fed to her, my friend swiftly consented to marry this man because she was raised in a rural, conservative community back in America, where she did not want to risk further shame upon herself and her family by being an unmarried mother in the 1990s. She now maintains in retrospect that her gut at the time strongly implored her not to take those vicious vows with him. She confessed that she was doing it for everyone else and what she thought they wanted for her.

Financially, he also detonated her life dramatically. He managed to deplete her entire bank account in less than 3 months after the marriage, broke the windshield in her car with a baseball bat in a fit of rage, threatened her male co-workers, harmed her beloved pet cat, and isolated her from her family, work friends, and colleagues with his mind games. Is this the way in which happy newlyweds should interact? No, but this man's sinister actions signify a typical script for a master manipulator.

> *"For there to be betrayal, there would have to have been trust first."*
> — *Suzanne Collins, The Hunger Games*

NASTY NARCISSISM: EXPLICATING CASE STUDY 1

Can you name at least three signs or features of covert manipulation and/or narcissism from the first case study scenario? How did he manage to build trust as the seed to his betrayal, as Collins' quote implies? I am sure your list may even exceed 10 at this point, but let us discover even more about case study 1 as painful and wretched as this exploration is. This scenario definitely demonstrates nasty narcissism at its worst. This man did not stop at those manipulative maneuvers mentioned above. It was almost like he gained momentum and power and then spiraled even more out of control after gaining this authority.

In addition, my friend also conveyed how the ex-husband became increasingly emotionally and physically abusive to my her by pushing her down a flight of steps, name-calling and bullying her profanities daily, choking her, fluctuating between a villain and a baby as he would play mind games with her, and committing other acts indicative of a classic horror film. When my female friend ultimately discovered that she was not pregnant in fact, the covert manipulator professed that he had loved her so much and wanted to take care of her medical needs, so he was driven to such drastic tactics and false claims to expedite their marriage; he also maintained that he had chosen those terrifying tactics to save her from other men in the local who might want to exploit her youthfulness and innocence. In a sense, he was almost blaming the victim for his sick stunts!

"To be in hell is to drift; to be in heaven is to steer."
— *George Bernard Shaw*

CASE STUDY CHAOS: LOSS OF THE STEERING WHEEL

Clearly, this hellish case study exemplifies how my

friend lost all self-love, control, health, happiness, peace, self-esteem and dignity when falling under the spell of this manipulator. She told me how she desperately wanted to annul the phony marriage right from the start when she started to see the signs of deception, but the local legal and cultural provisions in that nation about married foreigners hindered her ability to seek freedom. She had to remain essentially a prison in his realm of power and control for almost a year before finally receiving medical, psychological, and legal assistance to survive.

What is more, during that dangerous time, she lost over thirty pounds, suffered from many missed days of work, developed an eating disorder to control anything like food that she was able to regulate, and fell into a mental haze of chaos, depression, PTSD, and profound sadness. No one at work or back in American knew that she was living a lie and married to a monster. She compared her existence at the time to living in "hell on Earth!" In fact, she admittedly lived in silent agony under the tight, constant grips of this "gravedigger," as she called him during our last conversation.

"Some of us learn control, more or less by accident. The rest of us go all our lives not even understanding how it is possible, and blaming our failure on being born the wrong way."

— *B.F. Skinner, Walden Two*

Skinner's powerful quote is one that starts to question the exact roots of manipulation. Was this man born this way? What were his parents like? Did he experience war or other military exposures that made him so angry and deranged? We will later examine the nature/nurture debate thoroughly from both sides in **Chapter 7: Born This Way: How Narcissism Develops: Nature, Nurture, or a Combination?**

Accordingly, I will defer to my friend's story as one of the three main teachable case studies in this book, so you can begin to notice typical manipulative trends, indicative signs, important terms, and common tactics. I will include exercises or mini homework to stop and process some of this book's content and to make it even more of a toolkit for you. I know it is extremely upsetting and painful to discuss and revisit her horror story (and the other cases with similar, stark outcomes); however, my friend specifically gave me her permission to share her story to prevent others, both men and women alike, from following in her steps.

Besides, stories such as my friend's awful ordeal may seem like dramatic dialogues or poisonous plots from fictitious books and sensational movie scripts, but the characters are indeed real and all too familiar nowadays. Thus, we must work together globally to teach others how to prevent covert manipulation from robbing our lives, reputations, happiness, health, sanity, passion, love, time, and financial stability. What are your top 3 takeaways about manipulation from learning about case study 1?

> *"The most terrifying thing is to accept oneself completely."*
> — *C.G. Jung*

Although I am not a formally trained psychological expert or sociological guru, I have embarked on a significant self-study, self-acceptance, and self-love quest concerning this topic to ascertain credibility for this book. I further use Jung's above quote for a basis for my book's power and framework. I also have taken several classes in basic psychological tenets and communication fundamentals to prepare with the sole mission to help others not succumb to covert manipulation using evidence-based and relevant research paradigms. One barrier that I often find when trying to work through issues of mind control and covert manipulation when reading on my own is the jargon. Because my book contains many song and pop culture references, I wanted to flip the script on self-help as stifling or fluff-filled, so I hope you appreciate and enjoy my humor. This topic is so dark, so I wanted to add a bit more light as we tackle some deep subjects and concepts.

Without overwhelming you with too much with tons of psychological mumbo jumbo and theoretical frameworks, this book tries to instill positive psychology to give the *gift of re*silience to all readers. Just think of it as my early birthday gift to you! Now where is the yummy cake?

WHAT IS POSITIVE PSYCHOLOGY?

"Authentic happiness derives from raising the bar for
yourself, not rating yourself against others."
— *Martin E.P. Seligman*

Have you heard about positive psychology? As the above quote highlights, it is an approach that enables us to find our own authentic happiness, something that covert manipulation tries to rob from us so violently. What exactly does positive psychology help us to achieve and how can it protect us against schemers and scammers? As its name aptly infers, Bazzano (2016) in "Healing and Resilience" from *Therapy Today* overviews how the concepts of resilience, learned helplessness, and putting an end to victimology underlie the basic tenets of this theoretical framework. It basically means what its name suggests, so you do not have to be an Einstein to fathom it.

All of these basic premises are essential when dealing with covert manipulation. Generally, some of the top theorists who advocate it include Rogers, Maslow, Seligman, and others, if you want to do more self-studies on your own about it. You can also check out my extensive reference list at the end of the book to uncover more amazing resources. Luckily, there are no essay assignments, quizzes, or tests after reading this book-hooray for that!

BLOWING THEIR COVERS: BASIC OBJECTIVES. WHAT WILL I LEARN AFTER READING THIS BOOK?

Finally, this book teaches the following outcomes:

- Contextualizes major tenets of positive psychology and its basic theorists

- Summarizes typical mind control and manipulative techniques to better understand the minds and motives of covert manipulators

- Compares and contrasts the fine line between "good" manipulation and "evil" manipulation (influence versus manipulation)

- Investigates some pros and cons of being a narcissist

- Defines self-love and ways to achieve it in your own life

- Explains influence and motivation based on scholarly research

- Correlates how the roles of integrity and ethics relate to manipulation and influence

- Presents some ethical, effective, research-based tips and techniques to influence others, improve your life and help your loved ones.

- Understands the role of boundaries for self-protection

- Introduces the communicative technique of Socratic questioning

- Stresses the importance of self-care and self-awareness

- Suggests practical ways to use empathy on manipulators and when influencing others

- Discusses how to use the communicative tactic of mirroring in everyday life

- Briefly defines and characterizes narcissistic personality and how it can sometimes manifest in covert manipulation

- Explicates three case studies to better understand manipulation and mind control

- Characterizes toxic leadership and its basic traits

- Links narcissism and toxic leadership based on research findings

- Describes grandiose and vulnerable narcissist types and cites examples

- Offers simple strategies for you to take control your life autonomously and authentically

- Validates why protecting oneself against manipulators is vital

- Highlights the fine line between "good" manipulation and "evil" manipulation

- Explores the Peacock Paradox of Narcissism and Panther Prowling

- Instructs how to find positivity and rebound after manipulation

- Suggests ways to recover self-confidence after manipulation

- Overviews major steps of The LUCK Cycle and Formula

- Understands why covert manipulation is so messy and evasive

- Cites global examples of effective influences

- Highlights how self-love can potentially change the world

- Estimates how many people possess narcissistic traits

- Investigates the value of a shared vision when communicating effectively

- Reiterates why authenticity and empathy are so beneficial for influencing others

- Emphasizes how listening for inspiration can expedite influential power

- Explains how to use higher purpose when you influence an audience

- Validates why and how Oprah Winfrey was effective at influencing others

- Defines motivational interviewing

- Gives concrete, everyday examples of how to emulate Oprah's influential techniques

- Summarizes the Slick 6 effective influencers and sales techniques

- Focuses on the value of reciprocation when influencing others

- Describes the merits of storytelling and the power of peers

- Clarifies how to use consistency and likeability when influencing people ethically and effectively

- How to make jealousy work for you to influence others ethically and effectively

- Practical ways to celebrate your strengths

- Why posture is a powerful tactic to influence others

- Discusses the value of timing when influencing others

- Summarizes the merits of music, art, nature, and service as self-care strategies

- Lists practical, research-based strategies to regain self-confidence after manipulation

- Examines basic coping mechanisms for self-love and self-care

"You have power over your mind - not outside events.
Realize this, and you will find strength."
— *Marcus Aurelius, Meditations*

Power, pride, self-control, autonomy... All these words embody the true essence of this book. As the above quote depicts, I maintain how we must start to gain power and control over our minds before we can really transfer those skills to others. You have all the power right there in your own mind, body, and soul. I just have to pry it out of you a bit. This premise of empowerment and free will, too, permeates this book, as I guide you through some informal self-reflections and engaging self-discovery activities. Of course, all of them are optional, so feel free to pick and choose.

All in all, if you're old (or young!) enough to remember Janet Jackson's iconic 1986 song called "Control," then this message embodies the main scope of what I am basically trying to offer you in this book to protect and advance your own life: better control over relationships, increased self-esteem, improved health, genuine happiness, self-love, open mind, open heart, trusting soul, logical thinking, ethical influence, and communicative effectiveness.

Are you ready to take control over your life first and foremost? Do you want to learn how to spread those wings of resilience and strength? "Come fly with me," as that classic song suggests!

Chapter 1

OXYGEN MASK MANTRA: WHY DEFENDING OURSELVES AGAINST COVERT MANIPULATION IS ESSENTIAL

"Had blundered into the unlikely journey knowing nothing, breathing grief like a sour gas. Hoping for oxygen soon."
— *Annie Proulx, The Shipping News*

Chapter 1 will achieve the following objectives:

- Summarizes how and why the "Love is like an oxygen mask on a plane" analogy relates to defending oneself against manipulative people

- Introduces the role and practice self-care and self-awareness in guarding against manipulators.

- Explains why self-love is so critical

- Defines self-love is and ways to obtain it

- Recognizes why and how self-love and self-compassion can counter narcissist people from hurting you and your loved ones.

- Highlights how self-love can possibly change the world

As an avid world traveler to over fifty countries, I have admittedly and wrongly closed my eyes briefly and zoned out when the flight attendants started their mundane pre-flight demonstrations about airplane oxygens mask protocols. Does anyone else admit to this blunder? I have also largely ignored the seat packet safety literature during most of my journeys until I heard the poignant "Love is like an oxygen mask on a plane" analogy and really pondered its true message and deep implications. Now I definitely pay close attention to every word when I am receiving any directives on a plane or reading the seat pocket provisions, not only because they are polite, legal, and safe, but also because of the profound logic that's embedded within this mindful mantra.

In other words, if we fail to truly inform, protect, and guard ourselves in times of emergencies and strife by not placing our own oxygen masks on first and foremost, then how can we expect to have the energy, stamina, stability, and health to fully care for others? If you are a parent, spouse, grandparent, roommate, friend, sibling, student, nurse, first responder, or worker of any type reading this book, then this message is a possibly a "make or break" moment for you.

Since current society heralds this idyllic notion of a "martyr man or mama," compelling us to be self-sacrificing and out of touch with what it really means to practice self-care and self-awareness, I want you to keep visiting this oxygen mask metaphor. Does it strike a chord in your own life and responsibilities? In reality, we have to address our own needs first in order to ensure that we are healthy, safe, sane, financially secure, and savvy enough to then help others with their "masks" among the turbulent, frenzied flights of life. Are you wearing your oxygen mask every day or is lost amid piles of other people, pain, chores, excuses, lies, denials, things, to-dos, etc.?

LOVE YOURSELF TO LIVE!

"If you have the ability to love, love yourself first."
— *Charles Bukowski*

Bukowski's short quote is quite *tall* in relevance and truth. Similarly, think of this book today as a literary *mask* to arm you against the foes and woes in life. It is truly time to learn how to *love yourself to live!* You don't need to travel to gorgeous Italy for a glorious Venetian mask, because this book will enable you to shine your own unique personalities and approaches to life much more mindfully and psychologically aligned based on these findings and techniques. As a result, you will be better equipped to not only defend your colleagues, peers, neighbors, family members, kids, friends, and loved ones against covert manipulation, but you will be able to wholly protect yourself.

While many critics joke about Justin Bieber's redundant and corny lyrics at times, I have to give him major credit and props for his "Love yourself" lyrics because that's exactly what this book today is trying to espouse-minus the Biebs' tons of tattoos and shotgun wedding scandals, of course! Are you ready to sport the marvelous mask of self-care, knowledge, hope, love, faith, resilience, patience, logic, sanity, and safety after reading this practical book? I hope to allow you to inhale and exhale with ease and confidence after learning some of these basic principles and techniques today. Let us cooperatively explore how to love ourselves to live fully and authentically as we now discuss self-love.

XS AND OS: SELF-LOVE: WHAT IS SELF-LOVE AND HOW DO I ACHIEVE IT?

"Don't sacrifice yourself too much, because if you sacrifice too much there's nothing else you can give and nobody will care for you."

— *Karl Lagerfeld*

Self-love is one of today's biggest buzz words. I challenge you to see how many times you encounter it online or in person today. It is particularly prevalent in blogs and other self-help texts. Self-love is important, so do not dismiss it as merely hype. When we engage with a manipulator, we are prone to self-sacrificing, as discussed in case study 1. How does self-care defend us and why do we need it? Is it just about getting massages and chanting in some weird yoga clothes? No, self-care much more than merely a trending term since it truly gives us our *oxygen masks* to survive emotionally, physically, spiritually, economically, psychologically, socially, and sexually in a healthy, happily, and harmoniously manner.

At this year's 2019 annual SXSW Conference and Festival in Texas, for example, self-love was even the overarching theme for the entire event. What is self-love and what exactly does self-love do for us and our world? For starters, it guides us to redefine success as recent research from PR Newswire (2019) asserts, "We've been taught that we have to wait for and delay happiness and joy, that if we work hard enough now, one day success and happiness will come. And then when it doesn't, and we get frustrated - they call that a midlife crisis. Self-Love flips the equation around. We create happiness and joy first". We will now totally flip the script on manipulators and surround ourselves in self-love after learning empowering theories, techniques, tips, strategies from my book.

Does self-love mean sleeping until noon, golfing all day and watching *Game of Thrones* all night? Again, it is often a word that makes many of us (dudes, especially) a bit uncomfortable with its touchy feeling kind of connotations. Rest assured, though, because self-love is for everyone! Self-love is the notion that we make or break our own sense of happiness and well-being essential if we are not engaging in self-control, mindfulness, and self-care. It is a pretty easy equation: when we are proactive and happy, we are healthier and more successful. No math geniuses are needed for that one!

But self-love is not just about the individual level. Instead, there is a much larger communal dimension. Studies confirm that self-love actually fosters unity and collaboration since "And when we're happy and successful, it's easy to do the hard work necessary to contribute to humanity". Ah, now is that oxygen mask metaphor making sense?

"How you love yourself is how you teach
others to love you"
— *Rupi Kaur, Milk and Honey*

Self-love is not only proactive and protective, but think of it as instructive: it clearly sets the pace and tone to educate others how we want, need, and deserve to be treated, as suggested in the above quote. Why is self-love so essential in our world today? Besides the individual level, self-love is also embedded into the larger social fabric globally and can even possibly foster greater tolerance and social justice worldwide on a larger scale. Rev up for a self-love revolution!

In reality, studies find how self-love is not a magical pill or lucky rabbit's foot, but a plausible solution indeed "for many of the country's problems, including school and work bullying, daily stress and anxiety, and the epidemic of not feeling good enough. It's a new pathway for success. If we can spread this message of Self-Love, we have the possibility of truly changing the world". Do you really want to "change the world?" Rock on with the Eric Clapton tune! Which causes are you passionate about supporting and advocating?

First, let's work on empowering ourselves on an individual level and guarding against covert manipulation. **Chapter 2** will examine the fine line between "good" manipulation and "bad" manipulation.

To summarize this section, Chapter 1 emphasized the following objectives:

- Explained how and why the "Love is like an oxygen mask on a plane" analogy related to defending oneself against manipulative people

- Defined self-love is and practical ways to obtain it

- Validated why self-love is so critical

- Introduced the role and practice self-care and self-awareness in guarding oneself proactively against manipulators.

- Recognized why and how self-love and self-compassion can counter narcissist people from hurting you and your loved ones.

- Highlighted how self-love can potentially change the world

Chapter 2

UNDER THE INFLUENCE: INFLUENCE VS. MANIPULATION

*"God, how we get our fingers in each other's clay.
That's friendship, each playing the potter to see what
shapes we can make of each other."*

— Ray Bradbury,
Something Wicked This Way Comes

Chapter 2 targets the following objectives:

- Defines influence and motivation based on scholarly research

- Compares and contrasts influence versus manipulation with definitions, examples, and research

- Recognizes why covert manipulation is so messy and evasive

- Understands the "under the influence" implications of covert manipulation.

- Discerns the fine line between "good" manipulation and "evil" manipulation

As the Bradbury quote delineates, manipulators can use us as the clay to mold their maniacal creations. If we rewind back to case study 1 again, how is this quote applicable to the manipulator's tactics? He made her feel like she was "under the influence," and she literally was! Sometimes manipulators do not use chemicals to foster this feeling of "under the influence," though. They can use words and mind control to almost simulate as if we are under the influence of a drug or sick spell. How does it feel to be under the influence? No, we're not looking at your wild college days and spring break escapades from Daytona Beach or Ibiza! Please hide those pictures from my mother! If you have just finished another round of brewskies, margaritas, or happy hour cocktails, then you can aptly describe these "under the influence' sensations.

As such, when we are ensnared into a covert manipulator's web of deception, lies, seduction, and power plays, it often feels like we are literally "under the influence" of a foreign substance, drug, drink, or "Funky Cold Medina" because of the hazy feeling, out of body and mind fog, pervasive sense of helplessness, lack of reality, and other symptoms that we often experience. The fine line between "good" manipulation and "evil" manipulation is often a blurry one. No, we are not just talking about that catchy song by Robin Thicke, T.I., and Pharrell. Those guys are musical studs, eh? I really wish I had Pharrell's hat collection. Talk about some influential fashion choices and accessories, right?

Yet how does influence compare to and contrast from manipulation exactly? J. (2010) in "Control, Influence and Manipulation" featured in *Corridor Business Journal* distinguishes between influence and manipulation by citing how "Influence is perceived as legitimate and worthy whereas manipulation is regarded as perverse". Whether you label them as perverse, demonic, sadistic, or another other type of negative adjective, manipulators are definitely illegitimate in their inauthenticity and immoral motives, attitudes, thoughts, words, and actions. Go back to case study 1 and see how these definitions align with the ex-husband. Are you having any "aha" moments?

"You can con God and get away with it, Granny said, if you do so with charm and wit. If you live your life with imagination and verve, God will play along just to see what outrageously entertaining thing you'll do next."
— *Dean Koontz, Odd Thomas*

To further express the fine line between manipulation and influence, it is essential to really assess what conning involves and how manipulators excel at it, as mentioned in Koontz's quote. Likewise, Konnikova (2016) perfectly sums the blurriness that cons create on the line between influence and manipulation in the riveting article called "Cons" from *Skeptic*: "Whenever people ask if I've ever been conned, I tell them the truth:" I have no idea" (p. 26). Does this cluelessness resonate with you after trying to pinpoint why and how someone duped you or did you wrong? Like my friend in case study 1, who literally thought she was pregnant with the man's child, these manipulators can make everything so real, so vivid, and so believable, that we sometimes cannot disseminate facts from fiction.

Different from overt manipulation, this feeling of utter obliviousness is so common when we are talking about covert manipulation and getting conned. Although getting pickpocketing while visiting stunning Prague is a major sign of overt manipulation (also not one of my finest days as a tourist, to say the least!), why is covert manipulation so evasive? Recall some examples in your life to demonstrate this concept. Think of it as optional homework, so we can learn these objectives more practically and personally. Gosh, I've had more than I can count and even more, but I will discuss three main ones in this book as primary case studies.

What else do we know about manipulative people and con artists? Konnikova (2016) further goes on to elaborate how manipulation is quite messy business:

"I've never given money to a Ponzi scheme or gotten tripped up on an unwinnable game of three-card monte – that much I know. And there have been some smaller deceptions I've certainly fallen for – though whether they qualify as full-fledged cons is a matter of dispute. But here's the thing about cons: the best of them are never discovered" (p. 26).

In other words, covert manipulators are such "Smooth Criminals" like the M.J. song; hence, we often fail to ever realize that we have fallen into their traps. Instead of blaming the perpetrator, luck often enters the picture as validation. As Konnikova (2016) surmises, "...we simply write our loss off as a matter of bad luck" (p. 27). How do these research findings correlate with the military manipulator man in case study 1? Do you see any parallels so far or any signs of luck?

Luck was not an issue in case study 1. We are not talking about luck in the traditional sense of finding clovers and winning lotteries. I advise you to chill a bit on the luck topic, because this book will address some of those issues more extensively in **Chapter 10: Lucky Charms: An Overview of the Luck Cycle and Formula for Ethically and Effectively Influencing Others.** No bowls of cereal or trips to Shannon, Ireland are included, though. Check out the power-packed, life-changing tips!

Chapter 10 is a short one, so you can make yourself a snack, take a lap, or refill your cup of Joe. Chapter 11 elaborates on this idea of the Luck Cycle more extensively: **Chapter 11: Shamrock Yourself: Applying Tips from the Luck Cycle and Formulate: Strategies For Using Influence, Not Abusing Influence.** As you can see from this preview, I will add confidence, resilience, and knowledge as you *blow the covers off* any covert manipulators in your peaceful path of life.

Babies and Psychopaths: The Power of Influence and Manipulation

The two highest levels of influence are achieved when 1) people follow you because of what you've done for them, and 2) people follow you because of who you are. In other words, the highest levels of influence are reached when generosity and trustworthiness surround your behavior."
— *Dale Carnegie, How to Win Friends and Influence People: A Condensation from the Book*

I recognize how disturbing the title of this section is, especially for parents, but I had to include these extremes to make a point about the fine line between the power of influence and manipulation. You will later see in the next paragraph where this comparison derives from theoretically. Babies certainly influence us in such a sweet, adorable, innocent manner, and we love all the wee ones out there. Now those toddler years can get a bit more manipulative for sure as the tantrums manifest, right?

As far as psychological studies to clarify the differences and similarities between influences and manipulators, one of my favorite quotes from Flora (2011) in the "The Art of Influence" from *Psychology Today* . In particular, Flora (2011) cleverly compares how "Babies and psychopaths have one thing in common: They're excellent at getting what they want. Many of us could learn a thing or two from these creatures, tantrums and dirty tactics notwithstanding" While today's book is certainly not encouraging you to become an evil villain or a whining toddler in diapers, I firmly highlight how and why it is so essential that we look closely at the mechanisms and tactics used both manipulators and influencers to see which tricks we can keep and which ones we can tweak or guard ourselves against getting tricked. There are also no night feedings, messy eating experiences, or diaper changes required, so no worries there! You do not need to wear a bib while reading this book, folks!

In addition, Radde's (2014) article, "The Power Of Influence," also examines various crossover factors within the powers of influence and manipulation: "Even though the words are used interchangeably in conversation, influence is distinct from and contrasts with the methods and outcomes of manipulation. Influence is the process or action of producing an effect without apparent force or direct authority. Manipulation, meanwhile, is the practice of consciously or unconsciously employing devious, deceptive, or dishonest means to achieve a desired goal". Reflect closely on these last two definitions. Try to then recollect the last time when you really and truly wanted to influence your boss to get a pay raise, asked someone out on a date, convinced a friend to do something, persuaded a family member to buy you something, or encouraged a group to take a summer vacation together. Then identify some shady thoughts that may have emerged in your mind at the same time about how to achieve these goals manipulatively. Can you spot the differences? Do you now see where the blurred lines can frequently occur within the process of influencing?

As we forge ahead to **Chapter 3**, we will specifically learn how the role of ethics, morality, and integrity are critical for maintaining that line between "good" manipulation and "evil" manipulation accordingly. It all sounds like comic book talk, but it is definitely real life and highly applicable to all of us.

To re-cap, Chapter 2 achieved these basic objectives:

- Defined influence and motivation based on scholarly research

- Compared and contrasted influence versus manipulation with definitions, examples, and research

- Applied the "under the influence" implications of covert manipulation to one's life.

- Distinguished the fine line between "good" manipulation and "evil" manipulation

- Recognized why covert manipulation is so messy and evasive

Chapter 3

MIND YOUR MANNERS: ROLE OF ETHICS AND INTEGRITY IN INFLUENCE AND MANIPULATION

"It is also a warning. It is a warning that, if nobody reads the writing on the wall, man will be reduced to the state of the beast, whom he is shaming by his manners."

— Mahatma Gandhi, Gandhi: An Autobiography

Chapter 3 presents these basic objectives:

- Clarifies the roles of ethics and integrity in manipulation and influence

- Compares and contrasts definitions of influence and manipulation

- Breaks down case study 1 to better understand manipulation and mind control

How many times have you heard the old adage, "Mind your manners?" I bet my grandparents are reading this right now with smirks on their gentle faces. Gandhi's quote above also takes it even a step further to imply a more religious and spiritual implication associated with manners. Well, these proverbs clearly relate to integrity and ethics as far as influence and manipulation aptitude. They indeed play key roles in discerning between influence and manipulation as well.

Again, Radde (2014) reiterates in *Successful Meetings* how "influence improves professional effectiveness, increases credibility, and enhances relationships, building trust and confidence that increases the likelihood of future cooperation and collaboration. Manipulation may result in getting *credit*, but also imbues relationships with suspicion and guardedness, resulting in resistance, resentment, and revenge". For manipulators, there is always something to earn or win, it seems. They focus so intently on the end prize that they abandon all manners and morals in the process. Can you recall a relationship that started with someone influencing but then shifting into the manipulating lane?

In case study 1 of my American friend's saga, she later learned that the ex-husband received a higher salary if he married her (and even more cash if he had a child or dependent) due to the military stipulations. He was not only motivated by the thought of seizing a young, innocent, foreign woman into his den of lies, but he was also motivated economically and sexually. She also found out after the divorce that he had indeed preyed on other woman in similar circumstances both before and after her relationship with him, so a pattern definitely emerged. How else can we separate between one's desire to influence, persuade, motivate with one's needs and urges to manipulate, other than adhering tightly to our manners, ethics, and integrity?

Are you ready for some clock talk? Timing is also a major factor when we look at the common differences. When we want long term results, for instance, we should typically opt for influence, as it is more likely to stick and persuade in the long run. As far as general influence practices, Radde (2014) also specifies how they usually include an "open" agenda, increased data, and free choices.

In contrast, think of manipulative practices as the direct opposite: they tend to utilize "hidden agendas, limited data, and forced choice. Influence is a win/win, with concern for the other's outcome; manipulation is win/lose, caring little about the other's outcome", based on Radde's (2014) article. Using these research findings as a lens, my book is all about cultivating your winning streak over manipulation!

As mentioned, the first case of my manipulated American female friend further demonstrates how the monstrous man definitely had a hidden agenda, applied forced choice, coordinated his timing succinctly with her medical maladies, and other signs that align with major manipulation. Revisit a manipulative moment from you own life as a victim or instigator. How did timing contribute to the actions? See, you're already correctly detecting the signs already, so read on to become even more informed and empowered!

Chapter 4 will give us a *wild*, animalistic change of pace as we look at the peacock paradox and panther prowling animal metaphors to discover the definition of narcissists and how they operate. Ready to roar?

In sum, Chapter 3 achieved these main objectives:

- Clarified the roles of ethics and integrity in manipulation and influence

- Compared and contrasted definitions of influence and manipulation

- Offered examples from case study 1 to better understand techniques governing manipulation and mind control

Chapter 4

PEACOCK PARADOX AND PANTHER PROWLING: WHAT ARE NARCISSISTS AND HOW DO THEY MANIPULATE US?

"He's satisfied with himself. If you have a soul you can't be satisfied."

— Graham Greene,
Doctor Fischer of Geneva or The Bomb Party

Chapter 4's primary objectives will teach you the following:

- Identifies what a narcissist is

- Offers basic signs of how to spot a manipulator potentially

- Examines gender differences in manipulation

- Presents case studies 2-3 to further emphasize narcissistic mechanisms

Devoid of souls, lacking a sense of consciousness, and possessing zero empathy are typical traits of a covert manipulator. As Greene's quote expresses, these concepts will be addressed in relation to narcissism and its various mechanisms. As a result, this chapter describes what a narcissist is, how to spot one potentially, and how he or she tends to manipulate us using some engaging wildlife metaphors. We will also examine if there is a gender difference when looking at manipulators.

First, let us cover gender benders. While both genders can certainly be narcissists, Behary's (2013) book, *Disarming the Narcissist⊠ Surviving and Thriving with the Self-Absorbed*, claims how the majority of narcissists are typically males (p. 30). However, as I specified in the introduction, I have come across a ton of vile vixens who manipulated me big time based on cultural an age differences, socioeconomic disparities, lascivious motives, psychological control, and other reasons that I have yet to pinpoint. In turn, I really want you to shed all stereotypes and limited notions that only males or vagabond-looking strangers sporting dirty mullets and lurking in vans are manipulators. As you will later see in case study 3, some of the best manipulators are refined in outer guises of deception in stilettos, fur coats, and lipstick, too!

Let us now move from gender to animals. Are you wondering why this chapter has animals in the title? Yes, I will admit that I have a soft spot for fur friends. Do you know how people often refer to their spirit animals? In this case, I was inspired to liken a narcissist to a lovely, proud, and attention seeking peacock or dark, menacing, predatory, and highly attractive panther since both seem to share many commonalities with narcissists. Based on a finding from Young (2016) aptly called "All about Me" from the *New Scientist*, we may think consciously that we dislike narcissists, but research exposes how we actually tend to judge them as "more confident, intelligent and attractive than other people. This means they are more successful in job interviews, more likely to become leaders, and preferred by the opposite sex. There's even evidence that narcissistic artists sell more and get higher prices for their work". Think back to someone in your life who was a peacock or panther before his or her game was exposed?

CASE STUDY 2: BAD BOSS

"You never really learn much from hearing yourself speak."

— *George Clooney*

To illustrate these notions with another true story, I once had a brazen and selfish boss who was so charming at the interview, full of positive affirmations, funny jokes, shared my love and passion for sports, and attracted me with his stories about innovation and global business successes. He was a real peacock or panther as far as his work persona, so I was excited about working under his leadership. Moreover, I will refer to this story as case study for the remainder of the book.

Within two days of accepting the job, I realized that he had embodied a peacock paradox: his first impression of colorful charm hid his plumes of power hunger and pathetic control. He literally ignored, bullied, provoked, annoyed, and interrupted me when I was in the midst of a sentence, on a work-related phone call or email, in the moment of securing a make-or-break deal via a conference with loyal clients, and even mid-sneezes. Yes, this man had zero etiquette and was the worse leader I have ever seen, a totally different side than what his peacock appearance portrayed at the interview.

During my first week on the job, he treated me like he was hazing me into a fraternity. He never made eye contact, talked in loud, cursing sarcastic tones and word choices, and even made fun of my accents. His bullying tactics were not just limited to me. He bashed the female secretaries' personal and sexual appearances, made racist jokes, often stole cash openly from the company to buy himself personal coffees and snacks, and other employed other unethical, horrible, and illegal tactics.

In fact, this boss was so self-absorbed that he would constantly retort to us, "My stuff won't take long," which negated others and me. He always felt that his needs came before anyone else's. He even used to pound loudly on the bathroom stalls of the staff re-stroom when we were in there occupied because he felt his *business* was literally more important than our *business*, even employees' physical needs. It was nar-cissistic, disgusting, and a total violation of personal rights! As his story suggests, manipulators usually have no boundaries, no self-control, no remorse, no emo-tional intelligence, and no filters. Have you met any-one with a peacock paradox in your own personal or professional experiences?

> *"For the most part people are not curious except about themselves."*
> — *John Steinbeck, The Winter of Our Discontent*

Steinbeck's quote about selfishness is perfect for this next section because of case study 2 about the bad boss. It is also a relevant quote because it signifies how a lack of emotional intelligence, poor authentic con-nections to others, and empathy voids all usually cor-relate with major signs of the narcissistic personality type. I hear some panthers on the prowl already. Are you ready to further explore the jungle surrounding this personality type of narcissism a bit more? You won't need any bug spray, special gear, or SPF for this discussion. Let us zipline along and explore more about personality theory in user friendly terms.

What is a narcissist? How we do distinguish one? First off, studies by Geukes, Nestler, Dufner, Egloff, Back, Hutteman, & Denissen (2017) from the acclaimed *Journal of Personality & Social Psychology* find that a blend of contradictions is often what makes a narcissistic so puzzling and yet immensely fascinating at the same time. In essence, narcissists tend to present a sense of self that is both puffed-up but shaky in nature. Sounds definitely like a peacock to me!

As Young (2016) emphasizes, narcissism is a personality trait, "existing as a continuum on which all of us fall somewhere. Someone with an extreme form of the trait - narcissistic personality disorder - is not going to get ahead (unless becoming a dictator is a job option where they live)". Both case studies 1 and 2 convey how these manipulators merely acted to get ahead and advance their own agendas, without any positive regard for others or consequences in the painful process.

Can you also name a few other examples from these case studies to validate this personality trait?

Next, how many narcissists actually exist? Studies by Young (2016) estimate how roughly "1 and 2 per cent of people fall into this category. Move along the narcissism spectrum, though, and you get to the everyday variety that you might see in a friend or boss". Again, males are more commonly narcissists based on research findings overall. Yet my case study 3 in this book will later explain the real life tale of a female manipulator in the next section, so you can get an equitable, balanced view. How many have you likely encountered in your own life? How many more are out there like peacocks and panthers just waiting to strike? It is truly "a jungle out there" as far as personality types!

CASE STUDY 3: SINNING SAINTS

"I've never considered myself a femme fatale as I've never seduced anyone and ruined their lives. At least as far as I know."

— *Scarlett Johansson*

As this Scar Jo quote implies, yes, women, too, can function as covert manipulators. I have a personal example that will convince and sicken you. Grab those handkerchiefs and tissues for this one. My extremely active, positive, social, religious, and sensitive grandfather was living alone into his early 80s and wanted to hire an aide and housekeeper to help with some errands and to keep him company while most of us family members were at work or in school. We were a bit overprotective at first about his decision, but he was an extremely faithful man, still solid and able in his mental capacities and overall independence. He appeased our worries about want ads in the paper and strangers coming to the house when he quickly informed us how he met the perfect lady, a young, outgoing, friendly single mom of three kids, who also attended his church. He quickly felt such compassion and empathy for this woman and was immediately drawn to her as she was working three other jobs as a maid, waitress, and babysitter to support herself and her three children on one income. He even called her a 'saint' because he claimed how she could recite scriptures, had a shrine in her apartment, and always wore jewelry with religious symbols on her and her children.

They immediately bonded over their shared religious beliefs and struggles of living alone without a partner. This charming woman also told him riveting stories how she had formerly escaped extreme domestic abuse, poverty, disease, and gang violence in her native country of Guatemala before entering the United States illegally. She was the product of rape, so her life had been difficult, oppressive, and even marked from day 1, so he felt like a guardian to protect her and to kick start her transformation in America. Her tale was definitely gripping and emotionally compelling, but what she did with this story was nothing but despicable. I will call this story case study 3 and refer to it throughout the book as we acquire and apply these new skills, tips, tactics, and concepts surrounding the topic of covert manipulation and narcissistic personality types.

How did this *saint* execute such devilish and hellish deeds to my innocent grandfather? Well, within less than a month (damn, she was fast!), the young woman established a close connection with my grandfather, beyond merely cooking, cleaning, and caring for him and his poodle. They would sing hymns, study the Bible together, learn English, and engage in other friendly acts. She would also typically take her kids to his home when she was working for him, and they even started calling him "Pappy." She would ask him to translate stories from library books to her and her kids and she gave him a purpose as a mentor, friend, spiritual advisor, and father figure, not just an employer.

As mentioned, her storytelling tactics were a major persuasive mechanism that she used and abused to manipulate her sweet victim. She narrated her stories of pain, struggle, and strife to secure my grandfather's unconditional trust, love, attention, respect, and empathy. She then exploited her innocent kids as they, too, started to steal antiques, jewelry, food, medicines, and cash little by little with her, while my grandfather serenely sat on the porch, read his Bible so piously, or lightly napped. My grandfather did not discover this woman's awful antics until she manage to swindle over $35,000 from his savings account. The amount that she robbed him of collectively is still unknown to this day. Even more vilely, she stole his overall trust, dignity, faith, happiness, and health. He eventually succumbed to severe heart problems after falling into a dark depression when he learned that she and her kids had scammed him under the guise of friendship, religious, trust, love, and loyalty.

Where is the line in case study 3 that delineates manipulation from influence? How did she use and abuse her influence to manipulate my sweet grandfather? Based on what you know about narcissistic personality traits and the peacock paradox, react to this woman's actions, tactics, and approaches.

While research from Young (2016) strongly claims how covert manipulators are often self-absorbed - and potentially obnoxious, I would also add immoral since this woman also engaged in highly illegal and unethical practices. Chapter 3 examined manners, integrity, and ethics and how the inability to apply them can foster manipulation, and this woman definitely lacked them all and more!

As for all three case studies, are you also detecting how "obnoxious" definitely describes a boss who won't allow workers to engage in hygiene privacy; it also characterizes a sick, desperate man who drugged an innocent woman in order to conceive a child and advance his bank account and military career, right? Can you list other examples that align with the research to better understand these serious topics? Are you able to share some stories from your own experiences that make these notions "aha" moments?

While this chapter recognized the features and basic definition of what a narcissist is and how to spot one, Chapter 5 will amp it up a notch and introduce you to two main types of narcissists: grandiose and vulnerable narcissists. Keep the case studies in mind as we discover what these two types entail.

To reiterate, Chapter 4's primary objectives taught you the following:

- Identified what a narcissist is and signs of how to spot one potentially

- Examined gender differences in manipulation

- Presented case studies 2-3 to emphasize narcissistic mechanisms

Chapter 5

BEYOND ARIANA: GRANDIOSE AND VULNERABLE NARCISSIST TYPES

"Realize that narcissists have an addiction disorder. They are strongly addicted to feeling significant. Like any addict they will do whatever it takes to get this feeling often. That is why they are manipulative and future fakers. They promise change, but can't deliver if it interferes with their addiction. That is why they secure back up supply."

— Shannon L. Alder

Chapter 5 addresses the following objectives:

- Explains grandiose and vulnerable narcissist types and their common features

- Lists some historical figures who were narcissists

- Discusses sexual urges and lack of morality among narcissists

- Introduces the peacock paradox and panther prowling metaphors

- Characterizes toxic leadership and how to detect it

- Links narcissism and toxic leadership

Now we will move beyond Ariana Grande and discuss grandiose and vulnerable types of narcissists. Alder's quote earlier suggests an addictive quality to narcissism. Which of the case studies' manipulators do you feel had an addiction? How did power and control keep accumulating and exacerbating for these villains? Is there a one-size-fits-all version or template concerning levels and types of narcissists as a whole? Psychologists generally distinguish between two forms: "vulnerable" and "grandiose" narcissists. Again, I am not going to get too clinical, so my coverage here is just an introduction.

On one hand, Young (2016) comments how the vulnerable narcissists "believe they are special, and want to be seen that way -- but are just not that competent, or attractive. As a result, their self-esteem fluctuates a lot. They tend to be self-conscious and passive, but also prone to outbursts of potentially violent aggression if their inflated self-image is threatened". Can you think of someone in your own life who fits one or both categories? Don't point any fingers or say any names, despite the "Say My Name" Destiny's Child old school tune! Cyber nod if you can relate to what I am suggesting. Which of the case studies do you feel most aptly reflects this type and why?

On the other hand, what are some typical features of a grandiose type of narcissist? Afek's (2018) article from *Psychoanalytic Psychology* clearly alleges how grandiosity may be defined as "an unrealistic sense of superiority, which is not necessarily reflected in outward behavior. In this respect, I see the shy narcissist as typified by grandiosity just like the grandiose narcissist, even if he or she may seem to be timid and unassuming. Again, these traits go back to Adler's complex quote above. I bet you can also name at least 20 or more celebrities who presently fulfill this type, right? What about everyday people in your own families or social circles?

As far as historical figures to exemplify the two types, the infamous Napoleon Bonaparte was likely the grandiose type since he fit the bill in many ways. In general, these people are usually more confident, possess a strong belief that their superiority is "unshakeable, even when it's unwarranted. They can be pompous show-offs, but they can also be extremely charming. It is this type of narcissism that's more commonly found and studied in the general population - and seems more likely to bring benefits", based on Young's (2016) findings. That certainly sounds like the Napoleon complex to me.

Further findings from Young (2016) based on experiments from the University of British Columbia in Canada caution how grandiose narcissists tend to exude "a robust sense of personal agency, a feeling that one's goals and strivings are worthwhile". Think of narcissism as a psychological, internal game of tug-o-war. Hold that rope with all you might in this fight against manipulation!

This fight is also evident in other research studies recently. For example, Afek's (2018) article, The Split Narcissist: The Grandiose Self Versus the Inferior Self," in *Psychoanalytic Psychology*, suggests how the narcissistic personality is "characterized by the presence of two alternately dominant, dissociated self-states: the grandiose self and the inferior self". Are there any gamers out there? Where and how did this fight or split permeate in any of our case studies thus far?

"Narcissistic personality disorder is named for Narcissus, from Greek mythology, who fell in love with his own reflection. Freud used the term to describe persons who were self-absorbed, and psychoanalysts have focused on the narcissist's need to bolster his or her self-esteem through grandiose fantasy, exaggerated ambition, exhibitionism, and feelings of entitlement."
— Donald W. Black,
DSM-5 Guidebook: The Essential Companion to the Diagnostic and Statistical Manual of Mental Disorders

Similarly, grandiose narcissism is not only linked to charming people but also selfish, exploitative, and entitled ones. We will later use the above quote for inspiration when we talk about "Man in the Mirror" in **Chapter 9: Building Boundaries: How To Protect Yourself And Loved Ones From Covert Manipulators**. However, Donald Black's informative quote above forces us to understand the "all about me" emphasis that narcissists commonly exude.

Along the same lines, Young's (2016) "All about Me" article validates how and why they are more likely to make morally dubious or shady decisions:

"Looking at data on 42 US presidents up to and including George W. Bush, Ashley Watts of Emory University in Atlanta, Georgia, and her colleagues found that those rated higher for grandiose narcissism were judged as being greater presidents: they did better on rankings of public persuasiveness, agenda-setting and the initiation of legislation".

Interestingly, the same study also labeled these exact leaders as impulsive bullies. Presidential peacocks and panthers sound a bit right for many political figures, eh? Consider many of your leaders, bosses, executives, and politicians today and see if you can detect any feathers or furs?

MISSING MORALS: LACK OF MORALITY AND NARCISSISM

Going back to **Chapter 3: Mind Your Manners: The Role of Integrity and Ethics In Manipulation and Influence,** we can see the scaffolding here. Bob the Builder is back indeed! Lack of morality, according to Brunell, Robison, Deems, & Okdie (2018) in the article, "Are Narcissists More Attracted to People in Relationships Than To People Not In Relationships," is commonly associated with narcissists. Poor morals usually pinpoint major signs of grandiose narcissists since they crave drama and "...love to take advantage of others, typically experience less guilt for their transgressions, and are less ethical in their reasonings about their everyday behaviors that can be potentially harmful to others". Going back to the first case study yet again, this man has still never apparently apologized to my female friend, the victim! Remember how everything is a game to master manipulators!

SEX IN THE CITY (OR COUNTRY!)

Sexual prowess is also common among grandiose narcissists. Are all cheaters and adulterers narcissists? While not all are likely in these categories, Brunnell, Robison, Deems, & Okdie (2018) attribute how grandiose narcissists are much more sexually active and lascivious; they also seem to possess the following:

"Greater endorsement of casual, uncommitted sex, more lifetime sexual partners, and a greater desire for short-term mates. The desire for power and influence links grandiose narcissism and excessive or unrealistic sexual attitudes and behaviors; this includes sexual coercion among women and sexual aggression among men".

My former bathroom boss bully in case study 2, for example, was eventually terminated for sexual harassment of both men and women and photographing them in the restrooms, so these findings definitely seem to be based in real world relevance.

In addition, Behary (2013) also cites a strong link between narcissism and sex addiction in the book, Dis-

arming the Narcissist⊠ Surviving and Thriving with the Self-Absorbed (Vol. 2nd ed). Cheaters are definitely embedded in this category. Do you know a player in the romantic department? Well, he or she might be the grandiose type.

Studies further suggest how narcissists also self-report more frequent mate poaching, defined as behaviors that are "enacted with the intention of attracting someone who is already in a romantic relationship for a sexual encounter. Mate poaching? Peacocks? Panthers? Are you seeing my jungle metaphors come to life here?

Again, sexual prowess and mate poaching were behaviors present in case study 1. For instance, my friend also narrated how her ex-husband, a middle-aged adult man, was deviously caught trying to date and sexually exploit high school students when he was supposed to be tutoring them in foreign languages. More lies, schemes, and self-promoting... Can you find some current examples from online news, in your own hometown, local community, workplace, school, or family that align tightly with this research about personality types and typical behaviors?

"I shall always remember how the peacocks' tails shimmered when the moon rose amongst the tall trees, and on the shady bank the emerging mermaids gleamed fresh and silvery amongst the rocks..."
— Hermann Hesse, The Journey to the East

PEACOCK PARADOX: NARCISSISM METAPHOR

As suggested earlier, like the wild but lovely animals of proud peacocks described in Hesse's preceding quote, these birds and prowling panthers are so similar to narcissists in many ways as far as their motives, behaviors, and tactics. The people and animals both usually lure us with their natural beauty, charm, wit, intensity, and self-confidence. Psychological theorists further propose how there is actually a "peacock paradox." Kaufman (2011) from *Psychology Today* explains how they attract us like the plumes of a vibrant peacock; accordingly, "You can't help falling for them and by the time you've gleaned their true colors, you're hooked-and possibly hurt." See, I really did not make these animal antics up myself. This description perfectly summarizes narcissists' appeals and methods overall. Have you ever been attracted to any human "peacocks?" What was the outcome of the interaction? Was it a rumble in the jungle?

SHOOTS AND LADDERS: LINK BETWEEN NARCISSISM AND TOXIC LEADERSHIP

After looking at romantic, sexual, and more personal connections to narcissism earlier in this section to distinguish between the two types, please now put on your oxygen mask again securely and let us travel to the workplace. How do narcissists often become toxic leadership at work?

Reverting yet again to my story about the American female friend who was conned into the malicious marriage, her manipulator was extremely outgoing, popular, and endearing others, traits that many narcissists usually possess. Kaufman (2011) further alleges how manipulative bent can actually be a major

"Lever for social influence as much as for exploitation. This is why narcissism and leadership often go hand in hand. The fun-loving narcissist may enjoy widespread networking and dominating a social group not because they want to exploit every person in their path, but simply because they desire the positive reinforcement of others." Don't pull that lever!

In the same case study 1 of my American friend who was duped and drugged, her ex-husband was a high level leader in the military as well, one who was extremely respectful, humorous, clever, and reliable at work, even during his awful abuse of his wife behind closed doors. Manipulators love the game of "Shoots and Ladders" as the climb the ladder of success and then shoot everyone on their path, so to speak! I hope I did not tarnish that classic childhood game for you now. If so, I apologize!

LEAD POISONING: HOW TOXIC LEADERS FUNCTION

Do you know the physical symptoms of lead poisoning in one's home, school, or office? Well, these symptoms can also commonly encompass toxic leadership in the psychological sense, as in case study 2. Schreiber's (2017) article called "Poison People Caution" from *Psychology Today* also highlights how a leader who often says, "I'd like you to run that big meeting for me. It will give you a chance to show off everything I've taught you. Or the one who starts scrolling through his Twitter feed the moment you begin talking", can often denote toxic narcissism in leaders. Pause for a moment and honestly reflect: are you currently working for one or you a toxic leader? Have you ever faced a poisonous leader? What happened?

How can we spot a toxic leader? One commonality among toxic leaders is that they never take responsibility for their actions. In fact, a 2011 article in *Psychology Today* called "The Art of Influence" cited how these toxic leaders may even see themselves ironically "as trying to help you out". Talk about stuck on themselves, eh? Again, the woman in case study 3 professed repeatedly that she was helping my grandfather, even by robbing him. Talk about evil and toxic, right?

TOXIC LEADERS AND PEOPLE: HOW TO SPOT THEM

"There is no good and evil, there is only power and those too weak to seek it."

— *J.K. Rowling,*
Harry Potter and the Sorcerer's Stone

In addition to the signs above, how else can you spot a toxic leader or person? Rowling's quote cautions how weak people are sometimes unable to discern between good and evil manipulation. Therefore, I will highlight some toxic leaders' common features, so you can spot them more proactively, like the peacocks and panthers that they are underneath all that beauty and brawn.

As far typical signs of poisonous leaders, complainers and constant critics are often toxic leaders. Schreiber (2017) in *Psychology Today* further validates how toxic leaders usually do not accept "criticism, questions, or opportunities for change/reflection; they, too, either don't believe in positive feedback or fail to make time for it". Do you constantly feel nitpicked at work, never praised, and always an audience or target for a laundry list or litany of complaints? Well, you may be in a toxic organization. As advised earlier in **Chapter 1,** you will definitely need to arm yourself at all times with your oxygen mask first to stay sane and safe in these toxic situations.

Remember your worst teacher, mentor, boss, or supervisor? Bad bosses make our lives miserable, yet they someone how rapidly rise to fame and acclaim in many organizations to seize power and prestige. Likewise, Chamorro-Premuzic's (2015) article, "Why Bad Guys Win at Work," from the *Harvard Business Review Digital Articles* identifies various career-related benefits for people with personality characteristics such as psychopathy, narcissism and Machiavellianism due to their higher levels of financial attainment and enhanced competitiveness. So why do these bad guys/gals always seem to win? I encourage you to think back to my earlier example in case study 2 about the boss who was such a control freak that he even monitored our sneezes and bathroom trips!

Finally, erratic behaviors, high degrees of impulsivity, and lack of a middle ground also tend to characterize toxic people and leaders. Studies by Johnstone (2016) in *Leadership Excellence* fully confirm how many toxic leaders tend to…

"…vacillate between severe highs and lows. These energy shifts are exemplified by highly engaged and energized periods at work followed by doubt and emotional lows. Psychiatrists and researchers continue to find evidence that this lack of emotional middle ground is prevalent among executives".

If you have ever felt like you are dealing with someone on a yo-yo in the toxic leader realm, then this trait is likely a red flag!

Are you now feeling a bit more confident about how to detect toxic and manipulative people? We are just scratching the surface, folks, on how to spot covert manipulators and toxic leaders. For more specifics, we will later dive deeper into **Chapter 8: Perusing the Puppeteers: How To Spot a Covert Manipulator.**

As we transition now to Chapter 6, we will uncover the triple threat known as dark triad. While Darth Vader will not be appearing today, we will be entering a dark abyss, so please clutch that oxygen mask tightly!

All in all, Chapter 5 reinforced the following objectives:

- Explained grandiose and vulnerable narcissist types and their common features

- Listed some historical figures who were narcissists

- Discussed sexual urges and lack of morality among narcissists

- Introduced the Peacock Paradox and Panther Prowling metaphors

- Characterized toxic leadership and how to detect it

- Linked narcissism and toxic leadership

Chapter 6

THE DARK TRIAD OF MENTAL MANIPULATION

"The only thing necessary for the triumph of evil is for good men to do nothing."

— Edmund Burke

Chapter 6's sole objectives will address the following:

- Explores what the dark triad means

- Explains narcissism, Machiavellianism, and psychopathy

- Realizes the role of competitiveness in covert manipulation

- Understands the "All about Me" manipulator's mantra

Have you heard of the dark triad? No, it is not a new punk Goth band, a dark brand of lipstick or nail polish on the Parisian catwalks, or the latest installation of a popular *Marvel* comic turned mainstream movie. In fact, Kaufman (2011) argues in the "Peacock Paradox" from *Psychology Today*, how together with narcissism, "Machiavellianism and psychopathy form a cluster of distinct but related traits known as the "dark triad." Sorry, it was not that weird third wheel date that you recently went on with your best friend and his date or that strange drink that your buddy forced you to try on a cruise to Aruba!

STAR LIGHT, STAR BRIGHT?

What is the dark triad and is there anything bright amid all this blackness? As far as deceptive ranking, all members of this triad are pretty evil, but narcissists are actually "the gentlest star," according to Kaufman (2011). Of course manipulators can be both outgoing and/or shy, but research surmises how narcissism is linked much more tightly to extraversion than are the other two. Hence, we can infer then that narcissism…

"...may be the most positive, social, and outgoing component of this triad. And when narcissists do behave negatively and aggressively, they tend to do so in response to social exclusion. Machiavellian and psychopathic types are more hostile to physical provocation" (Kaufman, 2011).

Again, I challenge you to use these terms as a general guide when you are watching an action movie this weekend, going on a first date tonight, interviewing a new employee this month, or visiting your child's new teacher this semester. Do you spot any members of the dark triad?

YIN/YANG

In general, these deceitful people of the dark triad tend to excel not because they are wholly evil all the time, but "In part, because there is clearly a bright side to their dark side", according to Chamorro-Premuzic (2015). They exhibit clear overlaps between positive and negative personality characteristics, especially in areas such as "extraversion, openness to new experience, curiosity, and self-esteem are generally higher among dark triad personalities. Try to think of them like chameleons who can easily change and swiftly adapt their camouflaging colors to suit their specific surroundings and fulfill their unique but selfish needs. Be on guard for these yin/yang tendencies in others. I also want you to pause and pick any of the three case studies to recognize how dark triad traits were prevalent within the context of manipulation and malice.

"Life has but one true charm: the charm of the game. But what if we're indifferent to whether we win or lose?"
— *Charles Baudelaire*

GAME ON: ROLE OF COMPETITIVENESS IN COVERT MANIPULATION

As encompassed in the quote above about charm, the notion of games and competitions in life is extremely alluring to manipulators, often one of the foundations for their covert work. As such, dark triad traits tend to enhance competitiveness, if only by inhibiting cooperation and altruistic behaviors at work. Do you know someone who acts like everything in life is a game?

Please save the 2020 Olympics for terrific Tokyo, right?

As far as the nature of competition in covert manipulation, Chamorro-Premuzic (2015) further posits in *Harvard Business Review Digital Articles* how psychopathic tendencies often facilitate both the seduction and intimidation tactics that frighten potential competitors and captivate bosses". Talk about "Toxic" by Britney Spears, eh? To depict this concept a bit more, I actually have a relative who is so competitive, controlling, selfish, and narcissistic that he tries to regulate his elderly father's schedule, diet, clothing choices, reading materials, medical needs, television shows, phone calls, finances, etc. The elderly father is still in good health and sound mind. However, this controlling relative, the elderly father's sinful son, recently told all siblings that if the elderly father would pass away, none of the siblings are "allowed" to inform the other family members, friends, neighbors, or local media for a few days or until this son concedes.

I want you to think about this sick game: controlling someone in life is really bad, but even in death? Because the control freak son wants to handle everything, he is already dictating orders instead of enjoying his precious time with his father lovingly, peacefully and respectfully. It is not only extremely sad but highly morbid that people operate in such callous and delusional ways when they are major manipulators. Do you know someone who is in "game on" mode 24/7 and to an extreme, like the son in the earlier example? Overly competitiveness is a red flag to monitor, as we'll later explain in **Chapter 8: Perusing the Puppeteers: How To Spot A Covert Manipulator.**

ALL ABOUT ME: A MANIPULATOR'S MANTRA

By focusing on previous example with controlling the elderly father and others like the American friend's ex-husband in our first case study, it is evident that both manipulators clearly reinforce the commonalities how narcissists are highly effective, skilled actors and actresses. They are so effective at pulling those puppet strings as they desire.

As noted in the earlier section about mate poaching and sexual prowess, when examining their actions romantically, manipulators are typically much more successful in short-term sexual relationships since they prioritize individual gains and are highly adaptive at getting what they want to suit immediate desires and impulses. Research from Chamorro-Premuzic (2015) also cites how in evolutionary terms, dark triad personality characteristics "constitute the essence of the freeriding". They feel and act in an entitled, "all about me" manner.

As we soar into Chapter 7, we will examine if narcissists and manipulators are born this way or if environmental and sociocultural factors led them to these destructive choices and poisoned personas. If you are a Lady Gaga fan, then you will enjoy this next chapter.

Chapter 6's objectives taught the following:

- Explored what the dark triad is

- Explained narcissism, Machiavellianism, and psychopathy

- Realized the role of competitiveness in covert manipulation

- Understood the "All about Me" manipulator's mantra

Chapter 7

BORN THIS WAY: HOW NARCISSISM DEVELOPS: NATURE, NURTURE, OR A COMBINATION?

"Our first impressions are generated by our experiences and our environment, which means that we can change our first impressions... by changing the experiences that comprise those impressions."

— *Malcolm Gladwell*

Chapter 7 covers the following objectives:

- Analyzes the early roots of narcissism

- Examines the nature/nurture psychological debate

- Characterizes helicopter parenting and the links to narcissism

- Offers practical strategies to raise kids who are not manipulators

Gladwell's quote about first impressions is extremely applicable to this book's topic. Do we formulate our first impressions about others and how to interact with them in a genetic or environmental manner? What about the sociocultural factors? Are you familiar with the nature/nurture psychological debate? Well, Lady Gaga's "Born this way" anthem is such a great song and perfect for dissecting the roots of narcissism as far as their environmental or hereditary origins. When we question whether to blame nature, nurture, or a combination, a combination seems to be the standard consensus based on research and my own observations. Which side do you currently favor in this nature/nurture or combination controversy?

GENETIC JEANS OF NARCISSISM: NATURE SIDE

As far as the genetic side, let us first look at the genetic jeans, so to speak. Studies posit how narcissism is relatively stable over time, like all personality traits, but it certainly can change in many cases. In fact, it often…

"…seems to emerge at around the age of 7, when children can evaluate themselves as people and compare themselves against others. Twin studies, as cited from Young (2016), indicate how there is a genetic component, "although we don't know how many or which genes are involved".

If you are a teacher, parent, grandparent, social worker, daycare worker, or other who deals with kids, tweens, or teens, then these are some powerful studies to contemplate to ensure that we are not raising narcissists and mini master manipulators!

HOME ALONE: ENVIRONMENTAL INFLUENCES FOR THE NURTURE SIDE OF NARCISSISM

"Children have never been very good at listening to their elders, but they have never failed to imitate them."
— *James Baldwin*

On the nurture side, I want to elaborate a bit on the "Home Alone" side. Baldwin's quote attests to the power of modeling and nurturing on children, tweens, and teens, as well as the sociocultural side of influences. As such, today's popular parenting paradigm that sometimes encourages helicopter parents is often to blame for making kids feel more entitled and selfish.

Besides, Young (2016) also explicated a study from Ohio State University in Columbus where narcissism among the child subjects was actually cultivated by parents who tended to overvalue and over-praise their children; these parents also deemed their kids as more special and more entitled than others. What type of parent are you? What type of mentor or coach do you want to be? What is your signature style when influencing younger family members, step-children, neighbors, or siblings?

How does the nurture side contribute to manipulation? How can we *slow its roll,* so to speak? When children are overvalued, they may internalize the belief that they are superior to others, which then facilitates narcissism in many kids. Young's (2016) studies further allege how we can stop narcissism in parenting by reinforcing to kids how they are loved and cared for, not spoiling them to no end; in turn, a loving approach will typically internalize the belief that "they are worthy as a person – the core of self-esteem." Gift them with experiences, not things. This terrific technique is something that keeps me sane and from going bankrupt during holiday shopping.

Are we looking at more blurred lines? Yes, indeed, we are! When pinpointing how influencing and manipulating balancing act, it is clearly such a fine line. In particular, the difference between narcissism and high self-esteem is not clear-cut though, "and some psychologists argue that over inflated self-esteem is as much of a scourge as narcissism". What are some ideas that you have for parenting in the present to avoid raising manipulators?

How can we balance that line? Why and how does today's helicopter parenting paradigm promote narcissism when adults are often just trying to nurture, love protect, support, and our children? How do we build their self-esteem but not make them into monsters of manipulation and malice? Webber (2016) explains in

"The Real Narcissists Today" in *Psychology Today* how parenting styles, the influence of other relationships, and one's sociocultural environments can encourage (or deter) its development.

Try making a list of what you see at the park, when you are watching your nephews' soccer practice, or at the mall food court when families interact. For example, Webber (2016) portrays how positive parenting is when mothers and fathers are warm and affectionate, spend time with their kids and show interest in their activities, which lowers narcissism as "the children gradually internalize the belief that they are worthy individuals-the very core of self-esteem -and this doesn't spill over into narcissism". As a parent, uncle, step-parent, teacher, neighbor, nurse, coach, grandparent, or babysitter, how can you embrace these positive parenting practices today?

For starters, I urge you to respect but do not overindulge kids. Studies assert how parental practices that elevate children on pedestals can produce narcissistic "mini me" versions. How can a parent avoid raising narcissists? Webber (2016) further recommends how it is better for parents to say to children, "You did a good job," rather than, "You deserved to win" or "Why weren't you as good as she was"? Can you create some one-liners to foster these messages and to break the cycle of narcissism among kids, tweens, and teens today?

Besides watching our language choices and bank accounts, I also suggest embracing a "back to the basics" approach. I am not urging you to go *Little House on the Prairie* type of parenting, but be kind to unwind by turning off the nonstop digital, technology, and media portrayals, where kids see spoiled reality stars acting manipulatively and getting in some old-fashioned face time with families! Try giving the gift of real face time, not the app! Board games, puzzles, coloring, badminton, or charades, anyone? Cards? Unplug to remain a positive, mindful parent and role model for kids. Let us all *be kind to unwind* at least an hour or more each day in a healthy, proactive way!

In addition to taking a tech timeout, we can also take what I call a "bank break." By merely saying no sometimes to kids' overly materialistic and egotistical demands, this step is often a major way to lessen narcissism from exploding (and perpetuating throughout adolescence, young adulthood, and into the whole lifespan). It enables kids to develop empathy, a positive sense of self-esteem, true connection to others, and better service skills.

Chapter 8 will introduce you to some puppeteers, but not in the parenting or *Muppets* sense. I will give you some pointers, techniques, and tools to easily spot someone who is being a puppeteer and trying to manipulation your strings. Are you ready for the puppet show?

In essence, Chapter 7 provided the following objectives:

- Traced the early roots of narcissism

- Examined the nature/nurture psychological debate based on research

- Characterized helicopter parenting and the links to narcissism

- Offered practical strategies to raise mindful kids who are not manipulators

Chapter 8

PERUSING THE PUPPETEERS: HOW TO SPOT A COVERT MANIPULATOR

"Because to take away a man's freedom of choice, even his freedom to make the wrong choice, is to manipulate him as though he were a puppet and not a person."
— *Madeline L'Engle*

Chapter 8 aims to fulfill the following objectives:

- Advises how to recognize and control a narcissist

- Articulates signs of possible narcissists

- Offers typical red flag behaviors of manipulators

- Includes rhinos and cockroaches as manipulation metaphors

- Defines cold empathy commonly used by manipulators

Pulling the puppet strings, as mentioned earlier, denotes a solid sign that one is prone to manipulation and stripping someone of his or her individual freedoms, independent thoughts, or free will, as the introductory quote above entails. Although this list below is not a 100% diagnostic or foolproof one, it offers some basic tips for spotting a covert manipulator. One marker that Afek (2018) includes is that a narcissist tends to be "largely centered on the regulation of his self-esteem. Andrews (2019) also specifies that we can normally spot one by his or her overambitious nature, lack of modesty, and hatred of being questioned or challenged. Look at these traits of self-centeredness, overambitious, and lack of modesty. Reflect on your own current relationships to determine if you are seeing any signs yet or smoke signals, as the next section will explore.

SMOKE SIGNALS

Time to stop, drop, and roll! Since a narcissist will often take his or her time to carefully select one's words and actions for the smoothest impact, you'll need to be on the defensive as well. Carefully assess this person for any signs of possible smoke signals in the "too good to be true" sense.

In addition to deciphering verbal and written messages, also look closely at one's body language, eye contact (or lack thereof), gestures, tone, etc. When you are trying to read people, truly reflect and dissect if the person is seeking attention "because he or she is outgoing or he or she is more intentionally exploitative in one's objectives, which is behavior deemed as "Machiavellian and, at the extreme, psychopathic" (Kaufman, 2011). Again, stop and think about the three case studies. Can you list at least 5 smoke signals that are now apparent to you after acquiring these skills and knowledge?

Similarly, I have also documented some common red flag behaviors by manipulators using Schyns, Wisse, & Sanders's (2019) article, "Shady Strategic Behavior:

Recognizing Strategic Followership of Dark Triad Followers" from the *Academy of Management Perspectives*. These red flags or smoke signals are named in no particular order of importance:

- Makes fast, short-term–focused decisions without accounting for any of the possible negative consequences or long-term outcomes

- Chooses big, bold, and risky decisions; high degrees of impulsivity

- Questions authority figures, existing rules, and the status quo but does not like to be questioned by others, ironically; lacks reciprocity as far as criticism

- Bullies, blames, and/or criticizes others excessively

- Schemes for personal benefit; fosters one's own agendas above all else

- Keeps knowledge to themselves rather than open sharing with friends, family, lovers, colleagues

- Utilizes manipulation tactics to reach selfish goals

- Seduces others to live a "wild" life and/or into romantic relationships as if one is playing a childish game

"It's discouraging to think how many people are shocked by honesty and how few by deceit."
— *Noël Coward, Blithe Spirit*

What are some other basic ways to notice a narcissist's dishonesty and deceit since he or she is not likely to have an arm tattoo with "master manipulator" as a visual or sensory warning? I have also designed these additional reader-centered tips to further guide you for determining some common manipulation signs based on research and personal experiences:

- **Me, Myself, and I:** Like the sensational, addictive song by G-Eazy and Bebe Rexha of the same title, narcissists often show fervent feelings of grandiosity, superiority, and uniqueness. Go back to the bully bathroom boss example in case study 2 for one of the most evocative ones. Notice how he was so gross and god-like in his approach. He truly radiated a "me, myself, and I" mantra.

- **Heavenly Hosts:** Another tip for how to recognize manipulative relationships and to detect manipulators comes from Giacomin & Jordan (2015) as they conclude how many manipulators fall into self-enhancement categories and may thus view themselves as "superheroes" or "saints". Similarly, in the first case study, my female friend also discussed how her ex-husband claimed to be highly religious and ultra dedicated to his faith. Of course it was all bogus, but it caused us to take heed of this "saints" and "superheroes" cover. Do you also remember case study 3's "saintly" implication?

Andrews's (2019) article in NZ *Business + Management* similarly suggests how manipulators expect people to wholeheartedly believe what they say, no matter what, much like a religious doctrine, holy book, or ideology. Do you know someone whose religion is basically him or herself on a pedestal, demanding and commanding others to strictly worship and rigidly obey? Watch out for these false *heavenly hosts!* They are fuller of hype than Heaven!

- **Fortune Teller:** A manipulator can also typically read other people and easily work out their weaknesses, according to Andrews (2019). He or she will then put strategies into place to control one's victims. It seems like the first case study husband did this with my American friend as he saw clearly how she was struggling in her adjustment to the new culture and life, so he seized the opportunity to strike and execute his diabolical plans. Can you identify someone who acted like a fortune teller before working manipulative magic onto you in your own life?

- **Sage on the Stage:** Manipulators are usually the center of attention and hate being ignored (Andrews, 2019). The bully boss in case study 2 epitomizes this notion because he would not allow anyone or anything to take priority before him and his selfish needs. Do you know some-one who has to be the *sage on the stage* in eve-ry context, role, occasion, event, or situation?

- **Red Balloons:** Like the awesome 80s song, narcissists are like red balloons as they vividly steal the spotlight and also exude inflated egos. Like balloons, manipulators are always ready to pop at any time with their unpredictability since "They believe they are more capable than anyone else, even though they have no particular skills to do the job they are applying for or the talents required to manage people and/or projects" (Andrews, 2019). Do you know anyone right now whose ego is larger than his or her shoe size? Pop that balloon!

- **Too Late to Apologize: Song: Failure to Apologize:** Most manipulative people refuse to apologize since it is all about them and their inflated sense of righteousness. Leunissen, Sedikides, Wildschut, & Back (2017) in the *European Journal of Personality* reinforce how "Narcissism is characterized by little empathy for the victim, which reduces guilt about one's transgressions. One Republic's song of that same title is super sensational, but not in the context of manipulators who feel it's "too late to apologize" to us when they have wronged, harmed, misled, or tricked us!

Similar to the inability to apologize, manipulators also do not usually own up to responsibilities or accept any accountability for their actions. Manipulators often embrace a steadfast view that "Nothing is ever their fault. Someone else or the world at large is always to blame for all their problems" (Hoffman, Rippon, & Watt, 2018, p. 36). Can you identify someone who plays the blame game on everyone and everything else? I encourage to end that game and triumph over manipulation and malice using these how to spot steps and strategies today!

"It is a wise thing to be polite; consequently, it is a stupid thing to be rude. To make enemies by unnecessary and willful incivility, is just as insane a proceeding as to set your house on fire. For politeness

is like a counter--an avowedly false coin, with which
it is foolish to be stingy."
— *Arthur Schopenhauer,*
The Wisdom of Life and Counsels and Maxims

Rudeness and impoliteness seem, as the quote articulates, to represent the new norms sadly. From school shootings, bullying tweets, road rage, and other common occurrences mark the sign of the times. We rarely hear of these perpetrators taking accountability and showing true remorse for their awful actions. For this reason, low guilt, in turn, is commonly associated with unwillingness to apologize" (p. 385). Again, the "too late to apologize" sign is a major one to detect.

As far as a bit of homework, please rewind a bit to the case of my bully boss formerly in scenario 2. He never ever apologized to anyone even after losing his job and all professional certifications in the end. Andrews (2019) also cites how manipulators tend to be smooth talkers and highly skilled to talk their way into or out of any situation (p. 28). Can you name any smooth like butter talkers and banterers out there? What do they say? What are their nonverbal like? Do you see any signs? Try to articulate 3-5 "aha" moments.

Because this chapter is so practical in scope, I have also devised some additional signs to watch as you spot a potential covert manipulator in your own daily life:

- **Hot and Cold:** Like the perky Katy Perry pop tune, covert manipulators are usually rife with fluctuating, hot and cold tendencies, according to Geukes, Nestler, Dufner, Egloff, Back, Hutteman & Denissen (2017). Manipulators often drastically "alternate with feelings of inadequacy, inferiority, and worthlessness".

These erratic, impulsive, unpredictable behaviors result from the fact that narcissists tend to solely make decisions based on their own immediate wants and needs.

Instant gratification is another commonality among master manipulators. For example, research further finds that in schemers' cunning worlds,

"Whatever they want now is good and whatever they do not want now is bad. Thus, if psychopaths want sex and their dates will not provide it, then rape is good and the dates are bad. If people have money in their pockets and psycho-paths want it, then robbery is good and the victims are bad" (Hoffman, Rippon, & Watt, 2018, p. 36).

Again, I challenge you to go back to the three case studies presented in this book and then identify how these signs were quite visible among the perpetrators.

The hot/cold erraticism is usually part of the complexity, charm, and also conniving that these manipulators bring to our relationships. In turn, they keep us utterly confused and always on our toes, much like a cat and mouse game: they force us to struggle to figure them out due to their mind games. Do you know someone who makes you feel like a hurried hamster on a wheel or a hurricane, as you are constantly trying to discern his or her true intentions, desires, needs, attitudes, and so on?

- **Dream Team:** If someone claims to be an excellent team player but lacks concrete evidence to validate these assertions, then raise your guard. Bower (2011) from *Science News* attests that narcissists usually "sugarcoat how they regard themselves -- believing, say, that they're humble team players -- and assume others hold them in high regard". Not the sugar I want in my coffee! Have you ever worked with someone who was the total opposite of a team player, something that was the core of what this person claimed to be? It might be time to bench that person!

- **Green Day:** Although we are not summoning the band with the same moniker, cute Kermit the frog, or sustainable green efforts and advocacy, associated with Earth Day, narcissism is strongly linked with high degrees of malicious envy. Did you ever earn a scholarship, award, contract, or prize but then have a colleague, friend, family member, or partner exhibit hostility and resentment toward you? Where did you see jealously signs in any of the three case studies? Go back and look for this mean green marker.

- **Bored Games:** Speaking of games, do you know someone who seems to be bored, so he or she reports to playing games for pure entertainment value or just to pass the time in a sick way? Findings by Hoffman, Rippon, & Watt (2018) also allege how "bored" tendencies are often clear indicators of a manipulator or psychopath: "Due to their impulsivity and response inhibition, psychopaths may be easily bored, constantly seeking other stimulation during the interview. There are several strategies interviewers can use to keep psychopaths interested, such as trading out interviewers, changing topics, or letting the psychopaths take the lead, telling the interviewers whatever they choose about their behavior" (p. 36).

While I am certainly not recommending any CSI tactics, you can try modifying some of these techniques when protecting yourself from or determining manipulators. We all know how board games like Scrabble and Monopoly are awesome, but "bored" games totally suck! Steer clear of them in your daily interactions.

- **She's so Vain:** Self-promotion attempts are also major signs used by manipulators. Watch any of the popular *Bachelor* or *Bachelorette* shows and it is often so transparent to us as viewers outside the circumstances to discern who is there to merely promote one's modeling, acting, or music career and which contestants are truly seeking love. As Young (2016) suggests, "Self-promotion comes naturally to narcissists". If someone is stroking his or her ego 24/7, then red flag that tendency for possible covert manipulation in the making. Dude, that Carly Simon was way ahead of its time in truth and relevance, eh? As far as a reflective moment, consider your relationships presently.

Is there someone who soars on self-promotion? Think about ways to clip those wings!

- **Nails on a Chalkboard**: Just as irritating as nails on a chalkboard, narcissists also radiate an aggravating sense of interpersonal abrasiveness that is extremely self-centered and devoid of empathy. Which of the three case studies do you feel exuded this notion the most? Why? How?

- **Stolen Goods**: Is there someone at work or in your class who seems to consistently steal others' ideas and then pass these notions off as one's own? If things go wrong, does the same person always place the some blame on someone else? If these descriptions sound familiar, then steer clear of this person who is probably operating from stolen goods and kidnapped motives.

- **Friends in Low Places**: Are you a fan of that country crooner song, "Friends in Low Places?" Regardless of your preferred musical genres, friends in low places are vital to a manipulator's operational success in many cases. Peterson & Brewis (2017) exclaim in "When self-confidence is a curse" from *London Business School Review* how narcissists have a nasty habit of surrounding themselves "with people who tell them how wonderful they are. If they fail, it's someone else's fault." When you are trying to delineate if someone is a manipulator or not, look carefully as his or her social circle and friends, both real and online/virtual ones.

- **Game On:** While we mentioned this one earlier and will continue to highlight it as one of the most prominent features, covert manipulators often exude high degrees of competition and rivalry. They are always comparing and seeking to have the last word (and win)! Go back to the case studies in this book and see if you can label which were gaming the most, how, and why. Then transfer this knowledge to your own life to disseminate these gamers.

- **5 Alive:** In the lens of the Big Five personality traits, Young (2016) also maintains how "they tend to be extroverted, open and conscientious, not very neurotic and low on agreeableness". You don't need to be a psychology major to recognize the Big 5's personality alive implications!

- **Liar, Liar, Pants on Fire:** Pinocchio syndrome is commonly a sign of serious manipulation in the making or midst. Do you know a compulsive liar and embellisher? I have heard my share of some real doozies in my day, and I bet you have as well. Fan the flames by using this detection technique to catch a liar, liar before the fire!

- **Royal Treatment:** We are not trying to glow with a Meghan Markle sparkle. However, many manipulators act like they are royals in the typical manner that they are usually extremely charming, socially skilled leaders who like to brag and show off excessively. Brunell, Robison, Deems, & Okdie (2018) also contend that they typically view themselves as powerful and maintain power in relationships by keeping their partners guessing about their interests and commitments. Ever been duped by someone who was playing hard to get? Those nasty portrayals of some Disney princes definitely come to mind. Can you name others in your life or the media who think they deserve the royal treatment 24/7 and manipulate others to attain this sense of status and control?

- **Fab Firsts:** First impressions by manipulators are using stuff from fairy tales, aced interviews, and magical movies. However, research by Bower (2011) in the article, "Narcissists Need a Reality Check," shows how their façades typically turn sour quite fast and are fleeting. Recall your first encounter with a bully or manipulator who is presently plaguing your life. What was the first impression like? Do you see any pervasive patterns yet?

- **Fake and Bake:** Do you know someone who is shallow, superficial, and fake? According to Hoffman, Rippon, & Watt (2018) from "Interviewing the Psychopath: Part I. *Counselor: The*

Magazine for Addiction Professionals," manipulators often share the quality of superficiality. They tend to focus on themselves, their egos, materialistic gains, and monetary goals. Find those who are faking and baking!

"Seldom, very seldom, does complete truth belong to any human disclosure; seldom can it happen that something is not a little disguised or a little mistaken."
— *Jane Austen, Emma*

REVISITING ANIMAL ANTICS: RHINOS AND COCKROACHES: MORE MANIPULATION METAPHORS

After reviewing our tips for spotting a manipulator, I also have two more animal antics in the form of additional animal metaphors to share and compare with the dark triad message. Andrews (2019) maintains how narcissists are marked by their pesky persistence and ability to hide the truth; they "literally have the hide of a rhinoceros and the survival skills of a cockroach" (p. 29). Like animals and insects, human manipulators will also do anything to win and survive, no matter how brutal or ruthless they must become. Consider this book if you will, like a fun form of intellectual (but humane) pest control!

In sum, the best puppeteers of manipulation use common strategies, not masks, strings, or military weapons. First, they rely strongly upon empathy. While their empathy is fake, it's still doled out in heavy dosages. Research from "The Art of Influence" shows that manipulators are usually masters at figuring out what others want and need. For example, "Consider the highly charismatic individual, or even those master persuaders--psychopaths. Contrary to popular belief, psychopaths possess impressive powers of empathy: they can read and gauge others' feelings very well, but they do it dispassionately".

Next, experts call this ploy "cold" empathy. We can often spot a manipulator by the overloads of empathy, but it's what I blatantly call "half-assed" empathy! We will continue to emphasize empathy in the remaining chapters. As far as a preview to **Chapter 9**, I will deliver some practical and evidence-based approaches to protect yourself proactively and peacefully and guard your loved ones against manipulation. Are you eager to build more boundaries?

In summary, Chapter 8 stressed the following objectives:

- Advised how to recognize and control a narcissist

- Articulated signs of possible narcissists

- Offered typical red flag behaviors of manipulators

- Defined cold empathy

- Included rhinos and cockroaches as manipulation metaphors

Chapter 9

BUILDING BOUNDARIES: HOW TO PROTECT YOURSELF AND LOVED ONES FROM COVERT MANIPULATORS

"When we fail to set boundaries and hold people accountable, we feel used and mistreated. This is why we sometimes attack who they are, which is far more hurtful than addressing a behavior or a choice."
— *Brené Brown, The Gifts of Imperfection: Let Go of Who You Think You're Supposed to Be and Embrace Who You Are*

Chapter 9 applies the following objectives:

- Understands the role of boundaries for self-protection

- Introduces the communicative technique of Socratic questioning

- Stresses the importance of self-care and self-awareness

- Suggests ways to use empathy with manipulators

- Discusses how to use the communicative tactic of mirroring

- Learns an array of strategies for protecting against covert manipulators

- Applies practical techniques to case study examples and personal relationships to practice new skills.

Brown's significant quote is one that hits me the most in the heart and gut as far as the value of boundaries when trying to dodge manipulators and toxic people in my life. Yes, please believe me, I know that building boundaries is really tough, but it is beneficial work to foster resilience and healing. In turn, I have included some creative, research-based strategies for erecting

and sustaining boundaries to block covert manipulators from entering your life based on experts and my
own personal experiences and with this topic:

- **Humor Them:** No, this doesn't mean tell jokes
  like Chris Rock, Leslie Jones, or Tina Fey do.
  It means that with manipulative people, you
  can often appease and manage them by hu-
  moring their inflated beliefs that they are the
  "greatest person to solve a problem. You can
  guide them, shape them. Having them in your
  team can be a good thing" (Peterson & Brewis,
  2017, p. 19) sometimes. In turn, reflect back to
  the context of case study 2. How could you use
  humor with a toxic source in your own life?

- **The Blind Side:** Although it was a great movie, we are not talking about fabulous films
  here. Protect yourself and your loved ones by
  thoroughly checking your blind sides or spots
  ahead of time. As far as relationships, Kwan
  (2019) from *Harvard Business Review* recommends this helpful analogy: "If you want to
  change lanes safely while driving on the high-

way, you can't just look straight ahead, put your foot on the gas, and swerve.

How do you cruise with caution? You first have to look in your rearview mirror and take in the threats around you. Only then should you make your move". Where is a potential blind side that might be clouding your judgments with a manipulator in your life currently? Remember that blind spot's initials are BS, so totally remove the BS from your life!

- **Back Burner:** Although it is easier said than done in many cases, it is vital to try and ignore the manipulator since he or she craves the drama and attention. Block a manipulator's calls, texts, emails, and social media attempts; resort to a restraining order, if you have to do so. Since toxic people hate to be ignored, these tips are essential. As Andrews (2019) suggests, ignoring is a manipulator's worst nightmare. Literally turn the other cheek to a narcissist. Close the blinds, door, and padlock!

- **Spring Cleaning:** This tactic does not involve a map, broom, or dust pan. It urges us, though, to do a thorough spring cleaning to rid your live of toxic, manipulative, dysfunctional people. When you need to set boundaries, physical ones make for a great starting place. Think of this strategy akin to what Schreiber (2017) labels as the "zone of self-management" since it can regulate your exposure to nasty people.

In essence, research concurs how "The single most important thing you can do is minimize contact. If you work near a toxic person, ask for a rearrangement of desks. Never sit next to a toxic person", if at all possible. Did you ever have a close encounter of this kind? It is certainly far from kind, right?

To illustrate, I once shared a close cubicle space with a mean manipulator in a stressful workplace who made it virtually impossible for me to sneak a moment's peace, so I started to get creative about how to isolate myself physically and emotionally from him, like mentioning that I needed to work in a different area because the others were being loud, citing my desire to get some fresh air and work alone on the bench outside, and other furtive excuses. Spring clean for sanity and security in a creative, proactive way today! How can you use proximity and space to create a safe space for yourself against manipulators?

- **Lead a Horse to Water**: Nay, nay, nay! We aren't referring to any farming strategies or Kentucky Derby bets here. Johnson & Smith (2017) in "How to Mentor a Narcissist" in the *Harvard Business Review Digital Articles* suggest how it is so helpful to always lead with how you feel: because the narcissist lacks empathy, "such feeling-oriented disclosures can get the conversation away from who is to blame and refocused on the real problem". Cowboys and cowgirls will love this one!

- **Act Like Statue**: No, we are not talking about getting your best Tyra Banks or Heidi Klum model pose on, although those ladies are kick ass and gorgeous! When we suggest acting like a statue, it means to stand firm and steadfast against bullies and con artists.

As Andrews (2019) remarks,

"Maintain a positive outlook. If you are dealing with narcissists who derive pleasure from watching others suffer, then seeing the pain they cause will only egg them on to more aggressive counter-behavior. Don't look ruffled, even if you're feeling annoyed, and eventually that behavior will diminish in frequency."

- **Self-Care**: Take care of yourself first. Again, don that oxygen mask first. Studies from Johnson & Smith (2017) also urge us that in order to avoid burnout, set time limits on the frequency of engagement with a narcissistic person. Tick tock, you need to stop!

"Some people think only intellect counts: knowing how to solve problems, knowing how to get by, knowing how to identify an advantage and seize it. But the functions

of intellect are insufficient without courage, love,
friendship, compassion, and empathy."
— *Dean Koontz*

- **Make It Rain With Empathy**: Honestly, this one is super hard when you are dealing with super jerks! Research from Johnson & Smith (2017) clarifies how the chances are high that a narcissistic person is a wounded child at heart, so have empathy:

"All the bravado and arrogance amount to little more than a front for poor self-esteem and a real fear that they are worthless at the core. Try looking beyond the inflated self-assessments and demands for special recognition and catching a glimpse of the fragile house of cards that is the narcissist's ego. This might just stir your empathy".

As echoed in a (2011) article in *Psychology To-day*, contrary to popular belief, psychopaths possess impressive powers of empathy:

"They can read and gauge others' feelings very well, but they do it dispassionately." Dutton calls this "cold" empathy. The takeaway for everyone: Be strategic when considering another person's perspective. That makes you smart, not ruthless". Ready to alter your own weather forecast today to make it rain with empathy?

- **Memorize Mantras:** Manufacture a clever and objective mantra to counter manipulation and coercion. These one-liners worked for my when dealing with family members and work clients who were literally out of control. For partners and family, it could be as simple as "I love you too much to argue" in order to diffuse manipulation and chaos. What can you use as your go-to mantras for mindfulness?

Studies by Schreiber (2017) also support how these one-liners are extremely protective and effective when a toxic individual blames or bullies you: "I'm not going to continue this conversation if you're calling me names," or

"I'm happy to discuss this with you when you're calm".

I know it sounds a bit corny, but keep a piece of paper or a post-it with your mantras in a safe, secret place to keep you accountable. That tip worked for me until I really mastered my mantra confidence and the words finally became second nature! You will know when you have reached the mastery stage when the manipulators can predict what you are going to say before it leaves your mouth!

- **Support System:** Ensure that you have an adequate support system to detox and vent after any manipulative and toxic interactions. Gather your peeps and crews! Schreiber (2017) strongly advocates a support system with trusted friends and positive family members, "Especially if the toxic person is a spouse, relationships with people who treat you with respect can buffer you from stress and help balance your perspective". Who is going to be your

"Oprah" as far as a support system against manipulators and toxic people?

Besides, this support is also advantageous for validating your point of view, boosting your self-esteem, and counteracting isolation, all issues that can be impaired when a manipulator strikes. Who will be your lifeline or support system against con artists?

"The guarantee of safety in a battering relationship can never be based upon a promise from the perpetrator, no matter how heartfelt. Rather, it must be based upon the self-protective capability of the victim. Until the victim has developed a detailed and realistic contingency plan and has demonstrated her ability to carry it out, she remains in danger of repeated abuse."
— Judith Lewis Herman,
Trauma and Recovery: The Aftermath of Violence -
From Domestic Abuse to Political Terror

- **Man in the Mirror:** One powerful communicative technique to protect yourself against a master manipulator is to use mirroring, which involves carefully reflecting a positive appraisal of the manipulator and his or her basic worth using statements like "We're really lucky to have you here," "It must be hard for you when others don't seem to appreciate you," as demonstrated by Johnson & Smith (2017).

I challenge you to now pick any of the manipulators from our three case studies (or choose someone from your own life) and formulate at least 3 mirror statements to protect yourself. Practice makes perfect with mirroring!

Johnson & Smith (2017) further caution how it takes time and patience with this exercise as:

"You might initially frame arrogance and entitlement as unusual self-confidence. By mirroring back unconditional respect and acceptance of the narcissist, you might just lower defenses, thereby opening the door to some dialog and self-awareness".

Do not be so literal, as you do not need to actually bring your favorite mirror or razor for shaving. Bearded, bold, and beautiful!

- **AmTrack**: Arm yourself like an Amtrack and strive not to get derailed when dealing with manipulators. Stay steady. Andrews (2019) specifically cautions how

    "It's easy to lose your own sense of purpose or goals when a narcissist tries to take centre stage. You don't need to attend to everything this person says or does, no matter how much he or she clamours for your attention. Find the balance between moving ahead in the direction you want to pursue and alleviating the vulnerable narcissist's anxieties and insecurities" (p. 28).

    Stay solid on those rails by keeping those boundaries intact! Ticket to Boston, Baton Rouge, or Burbanks, anyone?

- **Bluff Against The Fluff**: As one of the most direct strategies for dealing with a manipulator, this one is slightly riskier and gutsier since it pertains to calling a narcissist's bluff, which may mean that you ignore the person, but it also might warrant that "You meet that bluff with a laugh at least once in a while. Without being cruel about it, you can point to the inappropriateness of the person's egocentric behavior with a smile or joke" (Andrews, 2019, p. 29). Ready to bluff against all the fanaticism and fluff? Use this one with special care because it is a bit more ballsy than some of the other tactics ones suggested.

- **Go Greek:** The use of Socratic questions provides another communicative tactic to both protect and build insights when dealing with manipulators and toxic people. Studies by Johnson & Smith (2017) in their work with how to mentor narcissists strongly advise how rather than directly confronting one's narcissistic behaviors, try to employ dispassionate Socratic questioning. If they complain that other people don't respect them, you can ask something like, "I wonder why so many people have that reaction to you?" You can also be more specific. You might say, "I've observed that some people seem to think you are arrogant.

Can you think of any reasons why people might see you that way"?

Try making up some samples ones to use with your partner, colleague, family member, or neighbor who has been a menace to you lately. Going Greek is empowering and effective!

"Trust thyself: every heart vibrates to that iron string."
— *Ralph Waldo Emerson, Self-Reliance*

Emerson's quote is really telling in the context of covert manipulation as it encourages us to engage in heart work or self-love. We must possess the utmost trust first and foremost within ourselves. Trust is like a vitamin that keeps us aligned, healthy, happy, and sane. All in all, trusting one's gut and always maintaining vigilance denote significant ways to prevent covert manipulators from scamming you. Interestingly, as mentioned earlier, self-care, too, is a protective mechanism. Being self-aware is major first step and something that I hope this book emphasizes clearly to you. Oxygen masks again, everyone! It is time for takeoff!

Additionally, what else can we do to protect ourselves and our loved ones against schemes and games? Communicating honestly is a must. It is also essential to avoid always being a "yes" person and consider your own needs, too. Young (2016) from the *New Scientist* uncovers how those who are overly nice and constantly of giving their time and energy to others may become "burned out, or get exploited or overlooked," perfect prey for narcissists. No more Mr./Ms. nice guy/gal all the time, ok? Find a happy medium!

As we fly into **Chapter 10**, we will offer a concise section on how to use the Luck Cycle and Formula to ethically and effectively influence others. There is no landing in the lucky city of Dublin, but we will do our best to give you *lucky* tips and techniques.

To review, Chapter 9's objective focused on the following:

- How to communicate honestly, ethically, and effectively

- Comprehended the role of boundaries for self-protection

- Introduced the communicative technique of Socratic questioning

- Stressed the importance of self-care and self-awareness

- Suggested ways to use empathy with manipulators

- Discussed how to use the communicative tactic of mirroring

- Presented strategies for protecting against covert manipulators

- Applied strategies to case study examples and personal relationships to practice new skills.

- Advised how to be more self-aware

Chapter 10

LUCKY CHARMS: LEARNING THE LUCK CYCLE FOR INFLUENCING OTHERS

"He was just a coward and that was the worst luck any many could have."
— *Ernest Hemingway, For Whom the Bell Tolls*

Chapter 10's objectives hone the following:

- Introduces the basic premise and 4 steps of the Luck Cycle and Formula

- Emphasizes the value of listening as a communicative skill

Hemingway's allusion to luck was largely personal and literary, not strategic or psychological in the manner in which I am proposing today. However, it all goes back to remind us how luck is in our own hands when it comes to self-care. Have you heard about the LUCK cycle? No, it's one something we take to Monaco, Macau or Vegas in order to win big at the poker tables. It is also not a new type of green beer brewing for upcoming St. Paddy's Day bashes, either!

Instead, Roberts (2017) from *SB Business Weekly* heralds the LUCK cycle and formula, a four-step social engagement sequence, for ethically and effectively influencing others with its four simple stages:

- Step 1. Listen for inspiration

- Step 2. Understand the resistance

- Step 3. Call to imagine

- Step 4. Keep listening

LUCKY LISTENING

"Most people do not listen with the intent to understand; they listen with the intent to reply."
— *Stephen R. Covey, The 7 Habits of Highly Effective People: Powerful Lessons in Personal Change*

Covey's short and sweet quote validates why we need to listen intently. First off, apply step 1 of the Lucky cycle to listen with purpose. Roberts (2017) also suggests basically the same tip in the form of simply listening for inspiration. This type of listening is all audience-centered and empathetic in nature. It opens minds and perspectives; at the same time, it seems to also solidify us as a trustworthy, compassionate, genuine authority to our audiences. This type of listening is a circle of trust and collaboration, not a linear exchange of power and information sharing. Are you ready to grab those Q-tips and listen with purpose?

Conversely, when looking at the dark side, one of the most compelling features of a covert manipulator is his or her ability to actively listen with diabolical intent, all with a façade of empathy. While listening is such a simple technique, why do we often fail to use it correctly? If you carefully review the four steps, the manipulative (maniacal) man in my friend's marriage scam from case study 1 was definitely listening attentively to her problems and vulnerability: he was also imagining quite a bit, as jumping ahead and noted in step 3! Now do you see how there is such a blurred line between influence and manipulation still?

What is the link between listening intently and influencing ethically or lack thereof? The LUCK cycle is actually a great tactic and reality checker for ethically and effectively exuding influence. In case study 1 with the evil military man, was he listening? What about the two other cases? Did the manipulators use listening with a purpose? If so, was the purpose ethical?

Although this chapter was short, it was an introduction to the larger discussion of how the Luck Cycle and Formula can improve your life and communicative skills. **Chapter 11** will give you even more tips to use it for increased confidence and influence. Let us now gather some shamrocks in the Luck Cycle!

Chapter 10's objectives achieved the following:

- Summarized the basic premise and 4 steps of the Luck Cycle and Formula

- Emphasized the value of listening as a valuable communicative and interpersonal skill

Chapter 11

SHAMROCK YOURSELF: THE LUCK FORMULA AND CYCLE: TIPS FOR USING, NOT ABUSING

Here's the thing about luck...you don't know if it's good or bad until you have some perspective."
— *Alice Hoffman, Local Girls*

Chapter 11's objectives encompass:

- Offers a more in-depth exploration of the Lucky cycle and formula

- Highlights the value of a shared vision when communicating effectively

- Reiterates why authenticity and empathy are so beneficial in influencing others

151

- Emphasizes how listening for inspiration can expedite influential power

- How to use higher purpose when you influence an audience

- Discusses how emotional intelligence enriches our ability to influence

Ready to *shamrock* yourself and shroud your life with some skills, concepts, tools, and techniques to use, not abuse, via the LUCK Cycle? Hoffman's quote linking luck and perspective really captivates what I hope to stress in this chapter. In other words, the LUCK cycle and formula can easily guide you to influence others ethically, if you utilize it properly. It is also a great way to protect yourself and your loved ones, to excel professionally, and to communicate efficiently.

First of all, Roberts (2017) also contends that it is essential to have a solid game plan. Know your objectives for what you want to precisely achieve since

"Without a firmly rooted inner game, even our most admirable attempts to influence others become reduced to manipulation. The LUCK cycle helps us transcend this trap to activate shared vision by clearing the windows of perception within our target audience".

Feeling lucky involves much more than leprechauns, my friend!

Remember how "game on" was a common tool used by competitive manipulators and toxic leaders? Well, you can adjust this mentality, so it is not ruthless in order to attain clear objectives via a solid game plan.

SHARED VISION

As mentioned in the case 1 of my friend's failed marriage, the manipulator did not engage in a shared vision; instead, he exploited her because he had his own nasty agenda. If we want to influence others, we have to apply a shared vision, like "If you scratch my back, I'll scratch yours" type promise of reciprocity and mutual understanding. Pause for a moment for a short exercise. Think about how prominent retail and chain stores with reward systems are so effective right now at influencing and sustaining us as consumers to make return purchases. What tactics did they use to facilitate a sense of shared vision? Which ones generally work for you as a consumer?

How can you use shared vision as an influencer in your future romantic, educational, social, work, spiritual, or economic interactions? According to a 2011 article in *Psychology Today*, "Whether you're lodging a complaint or trying to change the world, begin by considering the impact of your goal on someone--or some cause--beyond you". <u>This sense of unity and connection will help you to attain your influential goals.</u>

NO COPYCATS

*"The privilege of a lifetime is to become who
you truly are."*
— *Carl Gustav Jung: Authenticity*

Yes, I am still on my Jungian jam again as far as theorists because his psychological ideas are so profound and applicable to this book's main objectives. I also added another animal antic, if you are keeping track or a PETA member.

Besides shared vision, authenticity is one of the major prerequisites if we truly want to influence others deeply, effectively, and ethically. Obviously, in the case study examples, these manipulators lacked authenticity and were like creepy copycats from something they had likely seen on television or in a movie. In case study 1, the cunning man was using chauvinistic and evil tactics from a bad movie to lure the young, naïve, innocent American girl in a foreign land into his mind control. Do you see any signs of authenticity at all in cases 2-3?

Conversely, experts insist that when we influence others, authenticity is vital. Robert (2017) specifies how

"One must also be engaging to attract "…others from a place of deep sincerity and inspired conviction, in a spirit of service and shared self-interest (aka "inner game")".

Using emotional intelligence, social skills, and a genuine vibe, how can you win at your inner game when buying a new home, changing majors in college, trying to get a second date with your soulmate, and other situations? Aim for authenticity when you execute your influential goals.

MUSING: LISTENING FOR INSPIRATION

Again, why is it so powerful to listen for inspiration, step 1? Roberts (2017) further highlights how as we learn to listen for inspiration, our sense of social reality starts to truly shift:

"Instead of seeing people as targets, we see them as a mirror of ourselves. When we look at people this way, we have no desire to fix or change them. We see their inherent perfection and express our appreciation by reflecting this back to them. They then naturally light up in our presence and open to our message. No persuasion required".

Great "Mirrors" song by Justin Timberlake and powerful advice for influencing proactively! Man, do I wish I had that dude's money and swag, though.

Moreover, as mentioned in earlier in this chapter and in **Chapter 10**, listening is a core component of influencing ethically and effectively. Again, Roberts (2017) asserts how

"Make listening for inspiration your first order of business in your social interactions and watch what happens. The mere intention to think this way expands our presence and summons powers of influence unavailable to the persuasion-driven masses".

Remember that hearing is the physical act but listening encompasses a more holistic, mindful approach where we are absorbing, relating, empathizing, etc. Really focus the next time you are trying to convince or persuade something: do not just target your goals but truly listen for inspiration and to foster shared vision!

SHOES CLUES: EMPATHY

If this book had a drinking game, you would be extremely full of (or drunk from) your favorite wine, beer, coffee, or chai because I have now mentioned empathy a million times and will continue to keep emphasizing it. In sum, walking in someone else's shoes, boots, clogs, or flip flops will gain us major influential advantages. As far as using empathy ethically, a great 2011 article from *Psychology Today* also encourages us to "Be strategic when considering another person's perspective. That makes you smart, not ruthless". Walking in someone else's shoes is tricky but essential work for building empathy, my friend!

OUTER GAME: KNOW YOUR AUDIENCE

"I call him religious who understands the suffering of others."

— *Mahatma Gandhi*

Now that you know a bit more about the nitty gritty of the LUCK cycle and formula as far as the inner game, let us look outward at the "outer game." Gandhi's quote perfectly reflects the compassion, tolerance, and empathy that we need to have with others. Roberts (2017), too, advocates a similar set of advice by professing how influence cannot happen without explicating knowing your audience. Who are your demographics? Think like a marketer. Consider age,

gender, language, sexual orientation, political affiliation, lifestyle, culture, religion, race, socioeconomic
status, education, and other key factors. Who is your
audience?

How do we achieve this goal? It actually goes way beyond demographics and has a holistic slant. The outer
game is effective because it encourages us to speak to
others' "core aspirations, framing our vision as a call to
transcend past and co-create the future (aka "outer
game")". The outer game causes us to really hone on
our audience, release our own agendas, and focus on
the ones we are seeking to influence. Plan ahead for
your next goal to influence and see how you can work
the outer game with more gal or guy game!

GLOW STICKS: FIND OUT WHAT LIGHTS SOMEONE UP!

Are you ready to rock with some lights, camera, action? No disco balls are included in this step. However, this one, for me, closely relates to the other steps,
making them all cohesive and unified. Steps to mas-
tering the LUCK formula and enriching your luck

with influencing also involve discovering what lights someone up, according to Roberts (2017).

What does this strategy mean? Do I need a lighter or some fire? It means to go beyond the surface to extract someone's passion. Try to deeply read each person you are trying to influence by a glow stick type method. Discover what lights this person up. No candles or matches are required. It is not a literal glow stick that you'd use for a Bon Jovi concern, on the 4th of July, or at a hot club on Miami Beach or Cancun. Find out what makes the other person *glow* to tap into your audience on a really personal level.

Next, it is vital to also establish a field of listening, which then encourages them to share fully. Listening again? Yup. When we pinpoint their root sources of passion and aspiration, it further helps to find and cultivate common ground, which is so important when someone is showing reluctance or resistance to us about what we are trying to encourage or present. Dig deeper beneath the surface to see the source of any opposition, apathy, or uncertainty. Shovels, anyone? It is dirty sometimes but rewarding work in the end when we establish a field of listening. "Strawberry Fields Forever!" You are now going to be humming it all day and night!

SKY DIVING: HIGHER PURPOSE

"He who has a why to live for can bear almost any how."
— *Friedrich Nietzsche*

We all need a "why," as the preceding quote demonstrates. What is your why or higher purpose when you are trying to influence others. By the same token, what is your audience's higher purpose? Both sides of the coin must be ascertained. Aside from digging deeper, higher purpose helps to facilitate our influence. This tip does not involve sky diving, wearing wings like the Victoria Secret models, or proclaiming oneself as a saint. Manipulators do not truly care about their audience as human beings, so that is something that we as influencers must definitely do differently.

Are you eager to sky dive a bit more into the why and tactic of higher purpose? Studies insist how we have to operate with a sense of higher purpose; otherwise, Roberts (2017) indicates how we are merely "crossing into the manipulation line, which involves just figuring out what to say or do to influence others to achieve our goals". Higher purpose, to me, is also closely linked to the moral, ethical, and empathetic reasoning. Make sure there are no gaps when you are finding and asserting higher purpose. Mind the gaps, as they say in England! Let us fly mile high in our higher purposes!

Because you are now equipped with mile high skills to excel at communicating and influencing, we will now look at the famous example of Oprah Winfrey as **Chapter 12** guides us how to emulate her when influencing others.

To repeat, Chapter 11 targeted these objectives:

- Offered a more in-depth exploration of the Lucky Cycle, steps, and formula

- Highlighted the value of a shared vision when communicating ethically and effectively

- Reiterated why authenticity and empathy are so beneficial in influencing others

- Emphasized how listening for inspiration can expedite influential power

- Explained how to use higher purpose when you influence an audience

- Discussed how emotional intelligence enriches our ability to influence others

Chapter 12

EMULATE OPRAH: MOTIVATIONAL INTERVIEWING

"You teach people how to treat you."

— Oprah Winfrey

Chapter 12's objectives include:

- Explores why Oprah Winfrey was so highly effective at influencing others ethically and with empathy

- Explains motivational interviewing and how to integrate it in communicative situations

- Gives examples of how to emulate Oprah's influential techniques

- Cites research about her power of influence

How many of you remember Oprah Winfrey's riveting television interviews and smooth journalistic style? She truly fulfilled the ability to "teach people how to treat you," as her quote above reiterates. She openly disclosed how she was formerly the victim of sexual abuse, but she certainly did not allow manipulation to impede her successes or ability to influence others. Scisco, Biech, & Hallenbeck (2017) in *Compass: Your Guide for Leadership Development and Coaching* sincerely praise her as a

"great example of what an influential leader can accomplish at the highest levels. Through gradual expansion of her reach, she has attained a level of *influence* that can change national conversations and transform individuals into overnight success stories" (p. 2).

While this book is not about making you famous, it aims to offer you tactics to influence, which is something that she wholeheartedly obtained (and surpassed) without any limits!

Because this book has examined 3 cases of evil influence, let us now turn to an empowering, ethical, and effective example through Oprah's techniques. She eloquently and successfully "walked the walk" and "talked the talk" as far as how to treat, respect, value, and influence people during the duration of her television show. If you are too young to even know who she is, search online for some of her sensational throwback episodes to see her work her magic. She strongly exemplified one of the most effective interviewers and influencers of all times based on her humanistic and signature style.

However, what were so typical features of her influential style? One book by Lofton (2011) called *Oprah:* *The Gospel of an Icon* actually suggests how she deeply influenced with a blend and agenda of how "to learn, empathize, and celebrate." There was also a spiritual sense or dimension to her delivery. She led with ethics, authority, and empathy and gained massive influence worldwide. She greatly stimulated viewers' minds, hearts, and souls, something that we can all learn from and try to follow when we influence others.

Research further uncovers how her influence was attested by the fact that when

"Oprah liked, needed, or believed something, she offered her audience nothing less than spiritual revolution, reinforced by practices that fuse consumer behavior, celebrity ambition, and religious idiom. In short, Oprah Winfrey is a media messiah for a secular age" (Lofton, 2011).

While manipulators use and abuse this saint syndrome, notice how she channeled it ethically.

How else did Oprah excel at influencing others so smoothly and eloquently? Well, one strategy that she cleverly used was to figure out precisely what others needed, as mentioned in *Psychology Today* from 2011. Her interviewees desperately wanted a real, compassionate, yet objective listener when they were conveying their most challenging life stories, terrifying traumas, darkest secrets, and tough truths with the whole world. But her focus was always so firmly rooted in determining and addressing their needs first and foremost. How can you emulate Oprah when you are trying to influence and motivate others this week?

In addition, motivational interviewing is one tactic that we can try when seeking to influence others.

Communication experts from *Psychology Today* (2011) herald the use of motivational interviewing, a structured way of talking to people that gets them thinking about the reasons they might want to change. This technique garners trust and mutual respect. It also warrants us to devise and cite "creative ways in which your agenda meshes with another's is effective in many realms of persuasion".

Okay, I will admit that motivational interviewing is quite formal, as it is commonly known in the therapeutic world, but feel free to modify it to fit your own life and specific needs. Hey, it works wonders when trying to get your partner to take out the trash, convince your stubborn teen or tween to do his or her homework, or persuade your office mate to wear less perfume (or just wear some deodorant, dude)!

ARM YOURSELF WITH EMPATHY

"Whenever you feel like criticizing any one...just remember that all the people in this world haven't had the advantages that you've had."
— F. Scott Fitzgerald

Here is empathy again, so drink up if you are playing the game, as mentioned in the last chapter. Refill, please! Fitzgerald's quote reminds us how part of showing empathy relates closely with having tolerance and embracing a sense of diversity, two more merits that Oprah clearly achieved. Therefore, the gold cup of empathy goes to Oprah Winfrey for influencing others. Take cues from Oprah as she was (and is still) the queen bee of empathy for so many reasons.

Coupled with authenticity and a motivational inter-viewing approach, Oprah also deeply influenced and positively validated even the most reluctant interview-ees by arming herself with empathy. Studies in the 2011 *Psychology Today* article strongly praise empathy since it enables us to determine what others want. Even to this day when I am browsing a new book, I am still swayed to buy or read it if it has the Oprah Book Club seal of approval. Talk about a book buzz of icon-ic influence, eh?

As mentioned, my book covered authenticity and rec-iprocity several times, so you probably already know this pattern and power of influence. These characteristics are also traits that Oprah employed so efficiently. Her warm and respectful tone, for example, is heralded by Raspberry's (2004) article, "Inspired by a Real Wonder Woman," from *Television Week*. Raspberry (2014) specifically recalls how we need to follow Oprah's lead when we influence others and truly make a deliberate,

"conscious effort to mirror the warmth, compassion and respect Oprah shows her subjects. Following her example, I try to couple strength with sensitivity so I get the answers I'm after in a way that leaves my subjects feeling enriched, embraced and empowered. And if I've done my job well, I'm left feeling as if I've provided a medium by which their voices can be heard" (S14).

However, you do not need to be a journalist to integrate these excellent strategies. Try using them today when you are influencing someone to join you for a coffee, purchase something for your workplace, secure a new client, invite a neighbor to join you for dinner, and other goals.

As mentioned, tolerance and diversity are tightly linked to empathy. We need to accept all people, regardless of ability, disability, race, language, status, political or religious affiliation, educational level, gender, culture, sexual orientation, age, and other areas of difference. According to Raspberry (2004), these features greatly enhanced Oprah's immense influential ability as "Her greatest talent is, in my opinion, her ability to connect not only with different types of people but with all the different parts within each of us" (S 14).

Listening with intent, as I highlighted in **Chapters 11-12,** also represent some of Oprah's main skills. Raspberry (2004) also maintains how Oprah modeled for us how to ask the relevant, "deeper questions, both of others and of myself, and to recognize the truth when I hear it" (S 14). What other features or methods do you notice that Oprah utilized so effectively as an influencer?

In sum, try to walk in Oprah's shoes when you are trying to influence ethically. When we walk in another person's shoes, boots, sandals, or skates, we can truly understand what motivates, scares, challenges, drives, and cultivates one's actions, thoughts, beliefs, emotions, etc. Arm yourself with empathy when trying to convince your neighbor to lower his blaring music, urging your spouse to plan a date night, or securing a new deal with a big investor on a major work project or bid!

Just as Oprah offered some excellent persuasive and influential pointers, **Chapter 13** will provide some additional ones for you to apply to your own life and interactions.

Moreover, Chapter 12's objectives mastered:

- Explored why Oprah Winfrey was effective at influencing others

- Explained motivational interviewing and empathy

- Offered research to validate Oprah's influence

- Gave practical examples of how to emulate her techniques

Chapter 13

SLICK 6 PERSUASIVE POINTERS: HOW TO INFLUENCE EFFECTIVELY (AND ETHICALLY)

"To be persuasive we must be believable; to be believable we must be creditable; to be credible we must be truthful."

— *Edward R. Murrow*

Chapter 13's objectives encompass the following:

- Summarizes the Slick 6 effective influencers and sales techniques

- Focuses on the value of reciprocation when influencing others

- Highlights the merits of storytelling and the power of peers

- Clarifies how to use consistency and likeability when influencing people

Credibility is imperative for influencing other people, as the Murrow quote maintains. One of my most enlightened psychological self-studies thus far comes from the work by Dr. Robert Cialdini, the Regents' Professor Emeritus of Psychology and Marketing at Arizona State University, who studied effective influencers and sales techniques to gain influence. You were probably guessing that I would say Jung, right? Well, wrong!

In a nutshell (or a sales pitch), I call this list the "6 slick" since Cliffe (2013) references in the *Harvard Business Review* how Cialdini labels these types of strategies as

"...both effective and exploitable, depending on which side of the equation you inhabit. Use these classic salesperson's principles judiciously, and beware those who might use them on you".

As a result, so we can check ourselves before we wreck ourselves:

1. **Boomeranging: Reciprocation:** When we feel that there is an equitable sense of give and take, we are more apt to believe someone or do something. Cliffe (2013) offers the classic examples of in-store wine tastings: "We think we're coming out on top, but the expectation to give back is strong within us, and leads us to buy something". How do we make this step happen in real life?

Think about phrasing your words with "partners," "next time," "my turn," your turn," and other words to denote reciprocity. This pointer essentially means that "People will help if they owe you for something you did in the past to advance their goals. That's the rule of reciprocity".

Not only will you gain (and sustain) more influence, but you will also radiate more confidence and swag with this tactic. Research recommends how

"We're given serious persuasive power immediately after someone thanks us. So say something like "Of course; it's what partners do for each other" -- label what happened an act of partnership".

Team work makes the dream work, right? Speak and act so your relationships *boomerang* back in your hands!

2. **Story Glory:** Storytelling: regardless of your age, I bet that you can recall poems and stories from childhood because you performed plays about them, read them with a teacher who was so captivating and engaging, or saw them in vivid, sensory stimulation in gorgeously illustrated books or fabulously films.

Since storytelling is so linked to our emotions, memories and cultures, we can gain profound influence on others with our unique stories, according to Heath's (2012) book, *Seducing the Subconscious: The Psychology of Emotional Intelligence in Advertising.* Besides the actual contents of our stories, we must channel our inner Meryl Streep and Denzel Washington personas and acting to really hook and then sustain them with eye contact, vocal variety, articulation, gestures, facial expressions, etc. Story glory will bring you persuasive standing ovations! Which top 3 stories can you narrate to attract your audience? Yes, a bit of homework again here.

"It's not what we do once in a while that shapes our lives. It's what we do consistently."
— *Anthony Robbins*

3. **Bark or Meow for Consistency:** Just like a fur baby who meows or barks consistently every time she wants water or treats, people want to be seen as consistent in their actions, values, and steadfast beliefs. Cliffe (2013) offers this example, "So if you ask me to publicly declare my devotion to animal rights, for example, I'm more likely to donate money to PETA later". In turn, think about using words like "loyal," "regular," and other signs of consistency when you want to influence others.

4. **Prom King or Prom King: Likability:** As shallow and/or Kardashian as this notion may

seem, studies from Flora (2011) in the "Art of Influence" strongly attribute likability to greater ability to positively influence:

"If you like someone, you are more likely to say "yes" to her request. If she is pretty, you're even more likely. And if she compliments you, well, that works, too".

While you do not need to sport a tux, look like Zac Efron, or don a formal ball gown, appearances really matter! Put away those yoga pants, comb your hair (if you have some!), and change that Metallica tee-shirt ASAP if you want to influence someone professionally.

5. **Power of Peers:** If you do not believe this one, check your social media accounts for validation. It is evident that consumers today are much more influenced by their peers than consumers are by any experts. Think back to your last online purchase. I bet a few dollars, pesos, or Euros that you read some reviews first by other customers before entering your credit

card information, right? Cyber hands, please! Power to the people!

Research by Cliffe (2013) further credits the potent power of peers as a highly influential tactic:

"If you look at TripAdvisor or Yelp, you find that it's not travel writers or restaurant critics who are influencing others' choices. It's people just like you and me, who can now report on their experiences".

6. **Hotel California:** One of the most compelling examples uncovered in my research to validate the power of peers comes from sustainable efforts by hotels that have effecively influenced guests to reuse their towels in recent years. Want to go green, anyone? Cliffe (2013) admits how "Making an environmental argument was powerful, but what really moved the needle was hearing about the number of other guests who reused their towels". Now that's something to make a real splash about as far as

influence and persuasion, eh? Welcome to the "Hotel California!"

Although this chapter was shorter, it was full of persuasive appeals. As we glide into **Chapter 14,** I will uncover more makeover tips to influence effectively and ethically.

All in all, Chapter 13 facilitated these objectives:

- Summarized the Slick 6 effective influencers and sales techniques

- Focused on the value of reciprocation when influencing others

- Highlighted the merits of storytelling and the power of peers

- Clarified how to use consistency and likeability when influencing people

Chapter 14

MAKEOVER STEPS FROM MANIPULATORS TO INFLUENCE EFFECTIVELY AND ETHICALLY

"Example is not the main thing in influencing others. It is the only thing."

— *Albert Schweitzer*

Chapter 14 explores these objectives:

- How to make jealousy work for you

- Presents ways to celebrate your strengths

- Understands the role of posture when influencing

- Discusses the value of timing when influencing

- Cites ideas to tweak from manipulators to enrich your ability to ethically and effectively influence others

To repeat from Chapter 12, leading by example is something that we commonly hear and a vivid way in which Oprah operated. It is also echoed in the terrific quote above. Besides heavy doses of empathy and the other strategies from research, the LUCK cycle and formula, here are additional *makeover* tips from manipulators to positively influence others effectively and ethically that have worked for me in my own personal journey:

- **Jam With Jealousy**: Move beyond peaches, strawberry, cherry, and those jams. Make jealousy jam or work for you, not against you. Young (2016) strongly suggests that we need to control any malicious feelings of envy and instead cultivate "benign envy". Say what? Benign envy is fuel, not fire, so it uses another person's success to motivate you to achieve more, "rather than making you try to undermine them" or compete with another, as

Young (2016) posits. Jam with jealousy and make Nick Jonas' "Jealous" song proud!

- **Celebrate:** Go all out Kool N the Gang style and regularly "celebrate" your strengths. Think like a narcissist and do not be afraid to acknowledge your positive attributes. Give yourself some kudos! I like to keep a celebration drawer or jar to document my successes. You can also use a journal, scrapbook, vision board, or whatever suits your style. Bring on the celebration champagne!

- **Jolly Green Giant:** No, we are not suggesting going vegan or vegetarian. We are using the "giant" tip to "big yourself up", something that narcissists are great at achieving. Young (2016) explored this technique via studies from the University of Toronto in Canada as research uncovered that narcissists greatly inflate themselves and are keenly "aware that others generally don't think they're as amazing as they do themselves. They may regard others as too dim to recognise their brilliance, and this allows them to dismiss negative feedback as stemming from jealousy".

For me personally, I like to use tons of positive affirmations, motivational quotes (as you can see here in my book), posted all around my work station and home. I am also a big fan of self-help podcasts and books as well as self-talk (yes, magical "Man in the Mirror" type pep talks)! How can you *big yourself up?"*

- **Power Preparation:** Be strategic and power prepare. This suggestion does not involve dropping down into 1000 push-ups, fasting for days, living on green juices and chia seeds only, or chugging energy drinks for power. On the contrary, Young's (2016) studies strongly urge how taking 10 minutes before a meeting or job interview to think or write about a time when you felt powerful. "People who did this went on to fare better in a mock business-school interview organised by psychologists at the University of Cologne, Germany". Now that is what I call "the write stuff" to power up, people! What are some simple ways that you can infuse this strategy into your own life?

- **Back It Up:** Like eye contact, posture is powerful. Research shows the value in sitting up straight and erect. To illustrate, Young (2016) explains a study from Ohio State University in Columbus, where people who wrote down why they were qualified for a job while sitting up straight went on to actually "believe more of these reasons than people who wrote while slumped over their desks". Ballerinas and athletes will love this one!

- **Tree Tops:** Similar to posture, Young (2016) also summarized a Harvard University study that also associated greater degrees of influence with those who channeled the power of "power posing" and standing tall:

  "Volunteers who stood with their hands on their hips and shoulders back, or who sat with an open, expansive posture for just a few minutes before delivering a speech as part of a mock job interview performed better and were more likely to be selected". Apple, pear, maple, or walnut? Stand tall, ya'll!

- **Sizzle With Superstitions:** While this may sound super eccentric, Young (2016) encourages us to wear our lucky ties, socks, or charms. People who brought in a "lucky charm" to help them in a memory test at the University of Cologne did better than those without charms and also set higher goals for themselves. Why? They tended to feel more confident. Where is my lucky horseshoe? Jot down at least 3-5 ideas that you can use to sizzle with your own superstitions. Have fun and be creative!

- **True Blue:** No, not the Smurfs. Being true to oneself, having personal integrity, and being kind to others are also suggested tactics to earn influence and motivate positively. Think about your *true blue* core values. How can you ensure that you audience knows and feels them, too?

- **Take a Stand:** Be visible as narcissists surely are. Young (2016) then advises this technique "for anyone who wants to come across well at their next work meeting or shoot to the top of the promotion pile. Stand up straight, make eye contact, dress well, share ideas in meetings, don't be shy". Do not be a wallflower when it comes to influence, okay?

- **Clock Talk:** Timing is so vital. Narcissists are experts at pinpointing when to strike. Likewise, emulate them and play darts with time since Young (2016) reiterates how there are indeed valid times when people have to be a little self-ish and entitled – "for example, if you believe you have the best idea of anyone in a group". Let your ideas be an alarm to articulate your feelings, ideas, visions, goals, etc. The clock is literally ticking!

Now that you have acquired some makeover tips, you can rise like a phoenix from the ashes after manipula-tion and victimization, as **Chapter 15** will suggest.

Finally, Chapter 14's objectives targeted these goals:

- Explored how to make jealousy work for you

- Presented ways to celebrate your strengths

- Understood the role of posture

- Discussed the value of timing

- Gave ideas to tweak from manipulators to enrich your ability to influence others

Chapter 15

PHOENIX RISING: ACHIEVING SELF-CONFIDENCE AND RESILIENCE AFTER MANIPULATION AND VICTIMIZATION

"The phoenix must burn to emerge."
— *Janet Fitch, White Oleander*

Chapter 15 explores the following objectives:

- Lists researched-based and practical ways for achieving self-confidence and resilience after manipulation and victimization

- Summarizes the merits of music, art, nature, and service

- Promotes basic coping techniques for self-love and self-care

Like the phoenix metaphor from this amazing quote by Fitch listed above, we can all learn to rise from the ashes of anguish and despair as we "rebirth" after encountering a covert manipulator. While it is certainly not easy, this chapter highlights how it is totally achievable. In brief, I equip you with some research-based and practical strategies to gain more self-love and confidence. Ready to "Rise Up" like the amazing Andra Day song?

- **Musical Mania:** Unleash your pain stress through music. Sing, dance, or rap out your feelings! Find a song about positivity like Katy Perry's "Roar," and you can use it as your mantra. Allow music to heal and hype you up when you are down. Studies herald the power of music, as mentioned in the playlist suggestions by Bruner (2019) (https://time.com/5529914/spotify-valentines-day-playlist/).

- **Get Artsy Fartsy:** Like music, art is also cathartic. You don't need to be Rembrandt to benefit from the holistic healing and self-care from art like scrapbooking, Zentagle, adult coloring, painting, and other ideas. Bazan (2018)'s article, "Recharge Your Spirit," highlights how art is a mindful, almost a meditative way, to holistically and proactively cope with depression, anxiety, self-esteem, and other issues. Pass me the purple paint now, will you? Stay in between the lines, too!

- **Pay It Forward**: By visiting a resident in assisted living, cooking a meal for a friend who just had a baby, and engaging in other acts of service, we can focus less on our own woes and more on others. See, it's all about that empathy again. Take a drink! Reflect upon 3-5 ways that you can pay it forward and place the focus on another today in your healing process after overcoming manipulation.

Strive to engage in service to others. If you can recall all the positive features of Oprah's sphere of influence in **Chapter 12**, you can further emulate her in this service regard and deem it as one of her major sources of influence. Specifically, studies from Wilkins (2015) in "Celebrity as Celebration of Privatization in Global Development: A Critical Feminist Analysis of Oprah, Madonna, and Angelina: reinforce how paying it forward was so intertwined into Oprah's amazing style:

"Other than her own foundation, she funds, among others: Mississippi Animal Rescue League; Clinton Foundation—AIDS and Climate Change; Project Cuddle; Free the Children (building schools in developing countries); Charlize Theron's Africa Outreach Project; Heifer International; Peace Over Violence; Red Cross; Somaly Mam Foundation (devoted to ending sex slavery); V-Day (stop violence against women); Women for Women International; and Worldwide Orphans Foundation".

Of course you do not have to be as global or prolific as Oprah in this regard, but I strongly encourage to you take baby service steps or crawls!

"The mountains are calling and I must go."
— *John Muir*

- **Nestle in Nature:** No, this doesn't actually mean *nesting* with the critters, scaling Mt. Everest, or sunning on the beaches of Jamaica. I urge you to consider countering all the digital and technological overload with greater routines that nestle in nature: a walk outdoors, a stroll in the park, a hike on the trail, a jog, or other ways can positive and holistically recharge you with vitamin D, the sunshine vitamin, energy, appreciation, peace, and happiness. Self-care after manipulation is achieved when we nestle with nature! Just make sure you know how to pitch a tent!

- **Amazing Race:** Although the show with the same title is one of my favorites, I am instead suggesting that to bring back confidence, you can simply sign up for a local 5K. Run, skate, skip or power walk to make time for you! Get those endorphins buzzing!

- **Ditch the Tech:** Put down that tablet, silence the phone, and shutdown all electronic devices to find your calm. This step is so essential for healing and boosting self-confidence after dealing with manipulators. Get your Zen on, ya'll!

Make a plan or pledge to yourself in writing how you can ditch the tech today!

- **Write On:** Use journal writing, poetry, letters, and other forms of writing to "process difficult situations. Studies unveil how the "private pages of a journal are the perfect place to express raw emotions. It also gives the author something tangible to go back to if trouble arises again. What helped me make it through last time" (Bazan, 2018)? You might be the next best-selling author?

- **Cat Nap:** Hey, it works for Garfield. Use a power nap to find peace and self-care. Please no snoring! Start counting those zzzs, sheep, and stars! "Dream On," as Aerosmith sang.

To review, Chapter 15's objectives reinforced these following:

- Listed researched-based and practical ways for achieving self-confidence and resilience after manipulation and victimization

- Summarized the merits of music, art, nature, and service

- Promoted basic coping techniques for self-love and self-care

Conclusion

IT'S A WRAP: BLOWING THE COVER OFF COVERT MANIPULATION

"So, in the interests of survival, they trained themselves to be agreeing machines instead of thinking machines. All their minds had to do was to discover what other people were thinking, and then they thought that, too."
— **Kurt Vonnegut,** *Breakfast of Champions*

As mentioned throughout all chapters of this book, compelling studies in psychology, health, sociology, economics, and other disciplines clearly urge us to shed light on this imperative topic, especially since covert manipulation is everywhere. In fact, Young (2016) reports how narcissism is increasingly

"on the rise - in Western countries at least, according to a meta-analysis published in 2008. One of the main reasons may be that Western culture has become increasingly focused on the self rather than on relationships".

I challenge you to talk the first fifteen minutes of any current reality show, and you will see the scary results. Consequently, let us nail this narcissism trend based on my book's array of insights, tips, and suggestions to identify and overcome mind control and covert manipulation techniques.

In brief, I hope that you now have undergone an extreme makeover holistically to transform your mind, heart, and soul in a confident, empowering, and mindful way to block manipulators, increate your ability to communicate, connect, and influence, and to authentically engage in self-love. My main goal was to free you as readers from the shackles of the past and from the chains of covert manipulators. Instead, I wanted to arm you with strategies to identify, cope with, and combat mind control, so you can soar with radiance and resilience!

VICTORIOUS OVER VICTIMS' STATUS

"Winning isn't everything--but wanting to win is."
— *Vince Lombardi*

Just like the empowering message Lombardi's quote, we must possess an inner drive or determination to win. One of my favorite songs is from Macklemore and Skylar Gray called "Glorious," because it radiates this theme of triumph. Similarly, I want you to feel *glorious and victorious* in your battles against manipulators after reading this book, working with some of the case studies, and completing some informal challenges and exercises.

In review, this book urges you how and why to establish boundaries to stop serving as prey and victims to malicious, manipulative people and scandals. Regardless if you have faced manipulation or deception socioemotionally, spiritually, physically, sexually, and/or psychologically, this book intended for you to autonomously *blow the covers off covert manipulators*, so you can now better safeguard yourself and your loved ones proactively, peacefully, and productively.

As suggested earlier, take solace in the fact that even the word "victim" contains the empowering, resilient message of "I'm or I am." Practice saying and writing your pep talk pointers to remind yourself "I am brave," "I am invincible," etc. Be victorious over any victims' labels or statuses that you or others might have wrongly applied to yourself or your life.

As this book uncovered various theoretical summaries and resources about narcissistic personality theory, be mindful that manipulators are often elusive, erratic, and unstable. This book also presented some basic signs and feature of covert manipulators. For example, this book reinforced why and how they have trouble developing healthy relationships. They also tend to be highly aggressive if given negative feedback, according to Daniels (2018) in "A Fundraiser's Guide to Getting Narcissists to Give" from the *Chronicle of Philanthropy*.

PARENT TRAP: HOW TO AVOID RAISING NARCISSISTS

"It is time for parents to teach young people early on that in diversity there is beauty and there is strength."

— *Maya Angelou*

In review, I also provided a *blast from the past* by shedding light on the possible na-ture/nurture/combination roots of narcissism, so you could explore more about this fascinating topic on your own, especially connected to the framework of positive psychology and current parenting techniques. I really tried to give the *gift of re*silience to all readers through my examples, case studies, research, and per-sonal testimonies. I also delivered ideas for how to raise and mentor kids, tweens, and teens who are em-pathetic, not manipulators. How is that for a literary *Parent Trap* to ensure that you and the next generation do not get *trapped* into a narcissistic net of destruc-tion?

WORKING 9 TO 5: TOXIC LEADERSHIP IMPLICATIONS

"Each of us deserves the freedom to pursue our own version of happiness. No one deserves to be bullied."
— *Barack Obama*

In short, for everyone out there who has a job, is a student, or is subject to authorities, I also tried to cover some basics about toxic leadership as far as their mind control, communicative patterns, manipulative mechanisms, and so forth. Like the Obama quote above, I also touched upon how to deter bullies, but it is a topic for later books that deserves its own coverage. However, I presented some basic research, common traits, plausible protective tactics, strong communicative strategies, and other beneficial safeguards to help shield against toxic leadership, an epidemic that is hindering our organizations, schools, corporations, military, government, and other all facets. Many of my ideas are applicable across diverse context and situations, so feel free to divide and conquer. Tailor this book's advice to suit your particular needs as you move and groove more logically, rationally, mindfully, and holistically.

SIGN OF THE TIMES: AN ERA OF INFLUENCE

"It's in our biology to trust what we see with our eyes. This makes living in a carefully edited, overproduced and photoshopped world very dangerous."
— *Brené Brown*

Like the Harry Styles' song (Yes, I am a secret *fan man* on the down low!), this book also explores how we live in an era that is so rife with influence and persuasion. As suggested in Brown's compelling quote above, we are unable to escape the persuasive, manipulative, and influential messages from the media amid this era of technology. As a result, I also embedded some basic ideas and strategies in the book to better cope with the bombardment of persuasive appeals and manipulative messages. Are ready to get real in the sign of the times?

Soules (2015) vehemently advocates how for our own self-defense, we thoroughly need to understand "the *psychology of* persuasion and its weapons *of influence*" (p. 101). I would also add health, happiness, financial security, and sanity to that statement. Like siblings, manipulation and influence are definitely related. However, I hope that you take away from this book that influence is much more humane, collaborative, ethical, and moral. There are easy, effective, and practical ways to take manipulative tactics and tweak them to get what we want, protect ourselves, express ourselves, and empower ourselves accordingly. Revisit this book as a guide when you need to address these specifics goals, as this topic is not just a one-stop-shop! It's real and hard work!

MASQUERADE MOMENTS

"A mask tells us more than a face."

— *Oscar Wilde*

While this book was not designed to earn you any frequent flier miles or points, please be sure to remember the valuable oxygen mask metaphor and advice. Therefore, I want to enable you to take off the manipulators' false masks as you securely place on your own oxygen masks of self-care. As resonated throughout the book, swiftly grab and apply your oxygen own masks of self-care first as the best line of defense against manipulators, mind control, and schemers.

Why is self-care more than merely a buzz word of the times? In sum, it does not mean sitting for hours under salt lamps or submerged in floating water chambers to de-stress. It can take a variety of forms, as we grow and show lasting love from inside of us. Experts also embrace this notion how self-love is firmly built upon ideas that "We all deserve success. We all deserve to be loved. And we all deserve to be treated kindly, especially by ourselves".

This book attempted to hone your communicative and critical thinking skills, guide you how to build, sustain, and repair positive, healthy, relationships, and enrich your interpersonal confidence. It also highlighted how influence and empathy can be used ethically and effectively. There it is again for those of you in the drinking game subtext!

Now that you have your oxygen masks on your road to self-care and resilience, I hope you can manage and notice that fine line between manipulation and influence. I wish all of you happy reading, love, peace, health, security, happiness, and sanity on your journey to *blow the covers off* covert manipulation and protect you and your loved ones from harm.

Robert Moore

OTHER BEST-SELLING BOOKS
BY ROBERT MOORE

Body Language Training – the bestselling book by Robert Moore.

Think how GREAT it would be to impress people just with your movements, your positioning, your walk... without even saying a single word!

In fact, today you can discover the best HIGH STATUS positions used by "Alpha male" celebrities all over the world. I will show you how I trained my Body Language in order to attract and seduce any woman I wanted in the past - and how you can do it too, for the rest of your life!

What if I told you that with some tips, your standing position could become a real sign of POWER?

What if after reading this short guide, you will be able to attract the girl you want, just sitting in a DOMINANT position or walking like a real badass?

Trust me, body language is really that powerful. You should already know that human beings are constantly reading situations and other people so that, really quickly, they can know what category to put them in: low status, middle status, or high status.

It's just a survival mechanism, because you have to know who has the power and who hasn't. That's something that's been hardwired into us over thousands and thousands of years. So, most people don't trust words, because we've been taught from a young age to lie with them. They prefer to read those status cues through the body language: THAT is the honest signal of High-Status!

High status body language = high status person.

It's that simple, and we trust it. Once we make the decision or opinion about that person, it's almost impossible for us to break it. Therefore, your body language is the UNSPOKEN TRUTH

When you have a high status body language, people conclude that you are in CONTROL of your own reality. Remember this, my badass friend:

"The body follows the mind, but the mind follows the body even more."

Having a high status body language will make you have a high status mindset all the time: this can CHANGE YOUR LIFE FOREVER.

Now, this is what you'll discover inside Body Language Training:

Why a High Status Body Language is so important for your sex life, social life and career...

The 10 Foundational Principles of High Status Body Language - once you understand them, you'll never come back!

My best tips and tricks for displaying a powerful Body Language - always, no matter what...

The complete Body Language Training system that has changed thousands of lives - including Hollywood actors!

What your walk reveals about you - how to look way more confident than your friends and colleagues...

How to make sure SHE finds your walk sexually attractive!

How to be recognized as the leader of your group, in any social situation...

How to fix your posture once and for all - I'll show you how to stand and sit like an Alpha Male!

How to boost your own mindset and have unbreakable confidence everytime you go out...

How to control the interaction and attract any girl - even that ONE girl that had locked you into the Friendzone!

How you can get free drinks at bars and VIP tables at clubs - just by displaying Power and Authority through your Body Language...

My best Tips and Tricks on building CONFI-DENCE, CHARISMA and LEADERSHIP, in any social interaction!

...and much more!

Voice Training: How To Unleash Your Inner Badass Vocal Power With Vocal Exercises, Become A Leader And Get A Deeper Voice In 7 Days Or Less

Voice is one of the most important qualities of a leader.

When you have a POWERFUL voice, life becomes so much easier. Your social life will be much better and your business life will reward you so many times. Girls will be much more attracted to you... and if you're a woman, your voice will be the SEXIEST it is ever.

Just imagine yourself at a business meeting: you will be the most valuable guy there, because your voice will be so STRONG and COMMANDING.

Everyone will be raptured by your words.

Political leaders and actors were not born with a powerful voice, they TRAINED it up to that point.

In fact, you don't have a quiet voice, you simply trained it that way.

Now it's time to train it the other way around!

Here Is A Preview Of What You'll Learn In Voice Training...

Why A High-Status Voice Is So Powerful: how to make people know, like and trust you immediately...

The 5 Secret Traits Of A Powerful Voice: capture attention and hold it in a trance-like state every time you open your mouth!

Voice Training: mouth and voice strengthening exercises and tonality secrets used by Hollywood actors to command your audience's attention...

The Power Of Enunciation And Suspense: how to become a master storyteller who holds people rapt, fully engaged and hanging on your every word...

... and much more!

Eye Contact Training - How To Attract And Seduce A Woman, Increase Your Confidence And Become A Leader

What if I tell you that with some easy, powerful exercises you can get a deep, high status eye contact in just a few days? It would change your life, right?

Well, IT CHANGED MY LIFE. When you can handle the tension of a deep eye contact with everyone, you feel invincible. When you can handle the eyes of your boss, staring directly at them with confidence, then you'll stop feeling like his slave.

And with girls... damn, keeping a high status eye contact with girls it's completely GAME-CHANGING.

The techniques I show you in this book will make them chasing for your attention: they are so powerful, that even HOLLYWOOD ACTORS use them.

People will start doing things for you, they will start looking to you for decisions and, for the most part, they'll simply do whatever you say.

Remember this, my badass friend:

"With great eye contact comes great power, and with great power comes a lot of pussy."

Now, here is what you'll discover in Eye Contact Training:

Why a high status Eye Contact is so important for your life…

What a high status Eye Contact exactly is: one simple trick to deep, powerful, relaxed eye contact…

How to command complete control of your eyes and your attention: this SCREAMS high status to anybody watching…

Eye Contact Training: how to OWN your internal tension - Specific practices and exercises to train you how to handle tension inside and outside…

… and much more!

PS - MEN ONLY: don't forget your FREE bonus book!

You can find it at this link: http://bit.ly/7-untold-secrets

What are you waiting for? It's 7 Untold Secrets, my best-selling guide on women psychology, attraction and seduction.

Believe me: this stuff will change your life, you won't regret it!

REFERENCES

Afek, O. (2018). The split narcissist: The grandiose self versus the inferior self. *Psychoanalytic Psychology*, 35(2), 231–236. Retrieved from https://psycnet.apa.org/record/2017-44789-001

ANDREWS, A. (2019). How to Recognise and Control a Narcissist. NZ *Business + Management*, 33(2), 28–29.

Bazan, J. (2018). Recharge your spirit. *U.S. Catholic*, 83(6), 12–17.

Bazzano, M. (2016). Healing and resilience. *Therapy Today*, 27(10), 18–21. Retrieved from https://www.researchgate.net/publication/312949708_Healing_and_Resilience

Behary, W. T. (2013). *Disarming the Narcissist⌧ Surviving and Thriving with the Self-Absorbed* (Vol. 2nd ed). Oakland, CA: New Harbinger Publications.

Bower, Bruce. (2011). Narcissists need no reality check. *Science News, 180*(4), 16. Retrieved from https://onlinelibrary.wiley.com/doi/abs/10.1002/scin.5591800415

Brunell, A. B., Robison, J., Deems, N. P., & Okdie, B. M. (2018). Are narcissists more attracted to people in relationships than to people not in relationships? *PLoS ONE, 13*(3), 1–23. Retrieved from https://journals.plos.org/plosone/article?id=10.1371/journal.pone.0194106

Bruner, R. (2019). Knowing One's Worth Matters And Luckily Spotify's Valentine's Day Playlist Is Actually About Self-Love. *Time.Com*, N.PAG. Retrieved from https://time.com/5529914/spotify-valentines-day-playlist/

Chamorro-Premuzic, T. (2015). Why Bad Guys Win at Work. *Harvard Business Review Digital Articles*, 2.

Retrieved from https://hbr.org/2015/11/why-bad-guys-win-at-work

Cliffe, S. (2013). The Uses (and Abuses) of Influence. *Harvard Business Review*, 91(7/8), 76–81. Retrieved from https://hbr.org/2013/07/the-uses-and-abuses-of-influence

Daniels, A. (2018). A Fundraiser's Guide to Getting Narcissists to Give. *Chronicle of Philanthropy*, 30(12), 70.

Flora, C. (2011). The ART of INFLUENCE. *Psychology Today*, 44(5), 64–69. Retrieved from https://www.psychologytoday.com/us/articles/201109/the-art-influence

Geukes, K., Nestler, S., Dufner, M., Egloff, B., Back, M. D., Hutteman, R., … Denissen, J. J. A. (2017). Puffed-Up But Shaky Selves: State Self-Esteem Level and Variability in Narcissists. *Journal of Personality & Social Psychology*, 112(5), 769–786. Retrieved from https://www.ncbi.nlm.nih.gov/pubmed/27854443

Giacomin, M., & Jordan, C. H. (2015). Validating Power Makes Communal Narcissists Less Communal. *Self & Identity*, *14*(5), 583–601. Retrieved from https://www.tandfonline.com/doi/abs/10.1080/15298868.2015.1031820

Heath, R. (2012). *Seducing the Subconscious⊠ The Psychology of Emotional Influence in Advertising*. Chichester, West Sussex: Wiley-Blackwell.

Hoffman, N. E., Rippon, W. L., & Watt, V. (2018). Interviewing the Psychopath: Part I. *Counselor: The Magazine for Addiction Professionals*, *19*(4), 33.

J. (2010). Control, influence and manipulation. *Corridor Business Journal*, *6*(31), 16. Retrieved from https://www.corridorbusiness.com/control-influence-and-manipulation/

Johnstone, K. (2016). Are You A Toxic Leader? *Leadership Excellence*, *33*(11), 21. Retrieved from https://www.hr.com/en/topleaders/all_articles/are-you-a-toxic-leader-5-signs-you-might-be-one_iv3dua0z.html

Johnson, W. B., & Smith, D. G. (2017). How to Mentor a Narcissist. *Harvard Business Review Digital Articles*, 2–5. Retrieved from https://hbr.org/2017/09/how-to-mentor-a-narcissist

Kaufman, S. B. (2011). the Peacock paradox. *Psychology Today*, 44(4), 56–63.

KONNIKOVA, M. (2016). Cons. *Skeptic*, 21(1), 26–31.

Kwan, L. B. (2019). The Collaboration Blind Spot. *Harvard Business Review*, 97(2), 66–73. Retrieved from https://hbr.org/2019/03/the-collaboration-blind-spot

Leunissen, J. M., Sedikides, C., Wildschut, T., & Back, M. (2017). Why Narcissists are Unwilling to Apologize: The Role of Empathy and Guilt. *European Journal of Personality*, 31(4), 385–403. Retrieved from http://www.soton.ac.uk/~crsi/Leunissen,%20Sedikides,%20&%20Wildschut,%202017,%20EJP.pdf

Lofton, K. (2011). *Oprah⊠ The Gospel of an Icon.* Berkeley: University of California Press.

Peterson, R. S., & Brewis, K. (2017). When self-confidence is a curse. *London Business School Review*, 28(2), 16–19.

PR Newswire. (2019, March 7). The Self Love Revolution Comes to SXSW. *PR Newswire US*. Retrieved from https://markets.businessinsider.com/news/stocks/the-self-love-revolution-comes-to-sxsw-1028014133

Radde, P. O. (2014). The Power Of Influence. *Successful Meetings*, 63(8), 14. Retrieved from http://www.successfulmeetings.com/Strategy/Management/The-Power-of-Influence/

Raspberry, P. (2004). Inspired by a Real Wonder Woman. *Television Week*, 23(16), S14. Retrieved from

Roberts, J. M. (2017). LUCK: The Science of Transformational Leadership, Part 1. *SB Business Weekly*, 4. Retrieved from https://sustainablebrands.com/read/stakeholder-trends-and-insights/luck-the-science-of-transformational-leadership-part

Schyns, B., Wisse, B., & Sanders, S. (2019). Shady Strategic Behavior: Recognizing Strategic Followership of Dark Triad Followers. *Academy of Management Perspectives*, 33(2), 234–249. Retrieved from https://journals.aom.org/doi/abs/10.5465/amp.2017.0005?journalCode=amp

SCHREIBER, K. (2017). POISON PEOPLE CAUTION. (Cover story). *Psychology Today*, 50(3), 50–88. Retrieved from https://www.psychologytoday.com/us/articles/201705/how-handle-the-most-toxic-people-in-your-life)

Scisco, P., Biech, E., & Hallenbeck, G. (2017). *Compass: Your Guide for Leadership Development and Coaching*. Greensboro: Center for Creative Leadership.

Soules M. *Media, Persuasion and Propaganda*. Edinburgh: Edinburgh University Press; 2015.

The ART of INFLUENCE. (2011). *Psychology Today*, 44(5), 64–69. Retrieved from https://www.psychologytoday.com/us/articles/201109/the-art-influence

WEBBER, R. (2016). THE REAL NARCISSISTS. (Cover story). *Psychology Today*, 49(5), 52–61. Retrieved from https://www.psychologytoday.com/us/articles/201609/meet-the-real-narcissists-theyre-not-what-you-think

Wilkins, K. G. (2015). Celebrity as Celebration of Privatization in Global Development: A Critical Feminist Analysis of Oprah, Madonna, and Angelina. *Communication, Culture & Critique*, 8(2), 163–181. Retrieved from https://www.deepdyve.com/lp/wiley/celebrity-as-celebration-of-privatization-in-global-development-a-b5YIt0VJRo

Young, E. (2016). ALL ABOUT ME. (Cover story). *New Scientist*, 231(3081), 26–29. Retrieved from https://www.researchgate.net/publication/305080163_All_about_me

www.ingramcontent.com/pod-product-compliance
Lightning Source LLC
Chambersburg PA
CBHW030308290526
45785CB00001B/263